DATE DUE		
NOV 10 1996	DEC 02 2008		

Doubles, Demons, and Dreamers

An International Collection of Symbolist Drama

Edited, with an Introduction, by
Daniel Gerould

Performing Arts Journal Publications
New York

Library of Congress Cataloging in Publication Data
Doubles, Demons, and Dreamers: An International Collection of Symbolist Drama
Library of Congress Catalog Card No.: 85-60663
ISBN: 0-933826-77-X (cloth)
ISBN: 0-933826-78-8 (paper)

Printed in the United States of America

Publication of this book has been made possible in part by grants received from the National Endowment for the Arts, Washington, D.C., a federal agency, and the New York State Council on the Arts.

General Editors of the PAJ Playscript Series:
Bonnie Marranca and Gautam Dasgupta

Acknowledgements

Earlier versions of the following translations appeared in the following journals:

The Ballad of the Seven Sleeping Brothers in China, yale/theatre, VII, 1 (Fall 1975).
Jaws of Night, Performing Arts Journal, III, 2 (Fall 1978).
Pierrot Assassin of His Wife, The Drama Review, XXIII, 1 (March 1979).
The Wayfarer, Performing Arts Journal, III, 3 (Winter 1979).
Visitors, The New York Literary Forum, IV, 1980.
Requiem, Performing Arts Journal, VI, 1 (1981).
The Crystal Spider, Performing Arts Journal, VII, 1 (1983).
Death and the Fool, Poet Lore, Vol. 24 (1913).

Grateful acknowledgement is made to the following friends and colleagues who read the translations and offered helpful advice: Harry Carlson, Jane House, Aviv Oriani, Jeanine Plottel, Burton Pike, Robert Pucci, Elizabeth Swain, Michał Kobiałka, Rémi Villiers, Marc B. Weiss.

Contents

The Art of Symbolist Drama
A Re-Assessment

Daniel Gerould

I am only what I create. All that exists, exists only in my awareness.
Alexander Scriabin

The world is a reflection of your interior state.
August Strindberg

I am the god of a mysterious world, the entire world is in my dreams alone.
Fyodor Sologub

By the introduction of total subjectivity into drama—that mirror of a supposedly external reality—the symbolists imagined a new theatrical model, polyphonic in form and irreducible to rational analysis or univocal interpretation, and thereby opened the way for the subsequent avant-garde movements that have dominated the stage in the twentieth century: expressionism, futurism, dada, surrealism, and the absurd. The world, which realists and naturalists had claimed could be fully known and accurately depicted, was revealed by the symbolists to be pure illusion—a veil of fleeting appearances behind which were hidden deeper truths. It was what lay buried within the psyche and concealed behind the mirror that this radical new poetics proposed to explore. Problems of perception and epistemology subvert prior certainties as the arena of artistic representation moves from outside to within the human consciousness. The drama that emerges from such an aesthetic is more sacred—or sacrilegious—than secular, returning theatre to its ritual orgins. The locus of this visionary art is not the here and now of daily life, not what can be seen and experienced in our normal waking hours; rather it is found in man's eternal bonds to the unknown, to the mystery in man himself and in the universe as he journeys over the abyss towards extinction.

In striving to put on stage what common sense declared to be non-dramatic and un-dramatizable, the symbolists liberated playwriting from mechanistic notions of chronological time and Euclidian space, and they enlarged the frame of drama to include other worlds and other beings than those inhabiting the bourgeois theatre that was, in the words of one of its practitioners, "the echo of society's whispers" (Emile Augier). The future stage of the symbolists would be multiple, fluid, polyvalent, a point of departure for imaginary voyages into unchartered regions.

> The whole of humanity, anthumous and posthumous, is represented in it in all its conditions and professions. . . . Everything lives in this tragedy: animals, things, and even death. The latter is the principal reality, the principal character. Its presence can be felt even when it is not present.

So wrote the poet, playwright, and pioneer film theorist, Saint-Pol-Roux, in the preface to his interior drama, *The Lady with the Scythe* (1899), and the last part of his declaration could be applied to the entire corpus of symbolist writing for the theatre which is haunted by mortality, yet filled with a pervasive animism—hence the dualistic vision of life in death and death in life that is the central paradox of drama in the symbolist mode.

From our perspective of almost one hundred years, the assault on objectivity of dramatic form seems an essential first step—perhaps none has been as important—in the series of revolutions that have transformed the art of theatre from the turn of the century to the present. But until very recently there has been no awareness of how much is owed to symbolism in its role as ground-breaker. For reasons I shall attempt to explain, symbolist drama has constantly been disparaged and dismissed as something marginal both by defenders of the status quo and by proponents of a socially committed theatre dealing with topical issues. Despite the widespread revival of interest in symbolist painting during the past decade, drama in the same mode—which has such close affinities to the visual arts—has continued to be undervalued. I believe that it is time to reassess the contributions of symbolist drama to modern dramatic technique and stage practice.

At the first appearance of symbolism in the theatre in the 1890s, it was easy for powerful drama critics—conservative guardians of an entrenched institution—to ridicule the strange dialogue, frequent pauses, and lack of action and to insist that it was contrary to the very laws of the drama about which they knew so much. For these experts in the nature of the dramatic, theatre meant sharp conflict among clearly defined social and psychological types over the possession of material things: money, women, power, position; it meant celebrated actors whose colorful personalities made them stars; it meant an upper middle class audience who went to plays as couples and wished to see imitated on stage their own familiar salons and bedrooms and their recognizable problems of marriage and adultery.

Disdainfully rejecting the theatre of commerce and all its practicalities, symbolist poets and novelists wrote their plays for no existing audience or playhouse. By envisaging a lonely, hypothetical, and unknown spectator, these artists created the future possibility of an audience and a theatre transcending the furthest imaginable reach of their own times, even though their own works sometimes had to remain unperformed for many years. For such drama there were no fixed forms, prescribed rules, or current models to follow.

Maeterlinck spoke for all symbolist playwrights when he declared his refusal "to be satisfied merely to observe and portray the trivial, well-recognized truths, facts, and realities of life." And in *The Notebooks of Malte Laurids Brigge*, Rilke opposes the voiceless silence of real conflict to those tiresome third persons standing at the threshold of the truly dramatic who serve to produce insignificant and endlessly repetitive triangles. Instead of verification of the banal infidelities of husband, wife, and lover, the symbolists were concerned with the erotic itself, the principles of male and female in the universe, and the fundamental sexuality of all beings and things.

By the time of the First World War and Russian Revolution, many of the original symbolist playwrights and theatre artists had become associated with newer movements, and to the generation that came of age in 1914 the drama of Maeterlinck already seemed faded and remote from the actualities of modern life, characterized by frantic pace, mechanistic rhythms, and mass political action. To the socially committed critics from the 1920s through the 1950s, symbolist drama was a minor aberration and a dead end. Quite naturally the children disavowed their parents, and it took an entirely new generation—that of the grandsons and granddaughters—to perceive the symbolist roots of modern theatre. The influence of symbolism has been no less great for having been subterranean for many years—as witness its legacy in the plays of Beckett, Artaud's Theatre of Cruelty, Grotowski's *Akropolis* and *Apocalypsis cum Figuris*, Robert Wilson's operas, and Kantor's Theatre of Death.

In arguing that symbolist drama is the starting point of all modernist (and much postmodernist) theatre, I should stress that the full evidence has rarely been considered and that the perimeters have been too narrowly conceived both spatially and temporally. Symbolism in the theatre—as well as in poetry and painting—was a truly international movement and spread not only throughout all of Europe but also to North and South America and parts of Asia. And it came in successive waves, affecting new generations of writers and producing some of its finest achievements in its later phases in areas far distant from its initial Parisian base. When the Théâtre de l'Oeuvre closed its doors in 1899, symbolist theatre may have come to an end in France (although its impact certainly did not, and the plays of Claudel remained to be discovered decades later), but it was at this point that it began to stir in Poland and Russia. Likewise in Spain and Portugal, Ireland, Greece, Roumania, the Ukraine, Latvia, Lithuania, and India, symbolist theatre enjoyed a second life after having been declared dead in Paris.

Further, rather than being a reactionary escapist tendency (as it has often been portrayed), symbolist drama both in Eastern Europe, and in Ireland and India, was a progressive force, awakening a consciousness of national identity and protesting against the drabness of regimented modern life. In its quest for cultural roots, symbolism was liberationist and opposed to all forms of repression. For its themes and techniques, symbolist performance was drawn to folklore, church ritual, pagan rites, fairy tales, popular superstitions, and communal practices. It battled against all restrictions and limitations, including those that isolated theatre from the allied arts of painting, poetry, and music, and aspired to be a total spectacle encompassing all of life.

To illustrate all these aspects of symbolist drama—particularly its involvement with complex social, political, and historical issues—would require consideration of full-length works—by playwrights such as Paul Claudel, Stanisław Wyspiański, Lesya Ukrainka, and António Patrício—that cannot be accommodated in an anthology that aims at being comprehensive. This collection of dramatic miniatures is an introduction to symbolist poetics in the theatre. Since the symbolists conducted many of their most interesting experiments in the one-act mode, which well served their conception of a drama of stasis and mood, short forms offer an opportunity to examine the principal techniques and major obsessions of the movement, and this is what I propose to do in brief comments on each of the plays.

If the symbolist playwrights worked without recourse to pre-existing models from the currently available dramatic genres or styles of the standard nineteenth-century repertory, they did derive guidance from several precursors. Wagner's *Gesamtkunstwerk* or total spectacle and Mallarmé's "theatre of the mind" provided contrasting mirror images of symbolist performance. Nietzsche's *Birth of Tragedy* disclosed the ritual origins and sacred function of the drama. Poe's theory of literary composition and his practice as a writer of poems and tales revealed the means of achieving a single overpowering effect through the artful marshalling of images. The cult of retrospection, encouraging reversion to anterior forms, led the symbolist playwrights back to the medieval mysteries and moralities or to the masks of the *commedia* and figures like Pierrot and his Russian counterpart Petrushka. In their regression to "primitive" ages before the advent of realism, these artists confirmed the rule that to go ahead, the avant-garde always goes back. Finally, a powerful pictorial orientation made symbolist playwrights seek inspiration and visual corroboration for their images in the work of painters who were part of the same movement, often did stage design and costumes, and were themselves deeply theatrical in their art: Moreau, Redon, Khnopff, Ensor, Vrubel', and before them the Pre-Raphaelites, Goya, and the Flemish primitves.

*****

The failure of the old ways is experienced as the End of the World, the tidings of the new era as the Second Coming. We sensed the apocalyptic rhythm of the time. Towards the Beginning we strive through the End.

Andrei Bely

A turn-of-the-century movement that ushered in a new age as it said farewell to an old one, symbolism was Janus-faced, looking both backwards and forwards, concerned with beginnings and endings, committed to genesis and eschatology. Rather than the familiar intermediate stages of humankind's sojourn on earth—marriage and the family—the symbolists sought to dramatize first and last things. In their quest for ultimate sources, poets, painters, and playwrights returned to the shadows of pre-history when primordial man emerged from the slime. Or, obsessed with world destruction (like our own *fin de siècle* as we approach the year 2000), they envisaged the blotting out of the sun and the final extinction of life on earth. Atavism or apocalypse.

The creation of a modern mystery play was a symbolist ideal proposed by Stéphane Mallarmé and given impetus by Wagner's example in *Parsifal* (1882). Of all the symbolist mysteries, Strindberg's *Coram Populo! De Creatione et Sententia Vera Mundi* is the briefest and most darkly ironic. Written in French as the prologue to his autobiographical account of spiritual torment and religous conversion, *The Inferno* (1898), the Swedish author's abbreviated history of the Creation, Fall, Flood, and Coming of the Savior had first appeared as a play-within-a-play in the epilogue to the verse edition of *Master Olaf* twenty years earlier.

In Strindberg's demonic mystery, the world is an infinitesimal corner of an abandoned universe. Created out of divine boredom and malice, human life is given over to darkness and suffering and hurtles towards the abyss. Drawing upon gnostic myths in which God and Satan are portrayed as co-eternal brothers, Strindberg rehabilitates

Drawing of a Head by Rabindranath Tagore

Portrait of Alexander Blok
by Konstantin Somov (1907)

Portrait of Andrei Bely by Leon Bakst

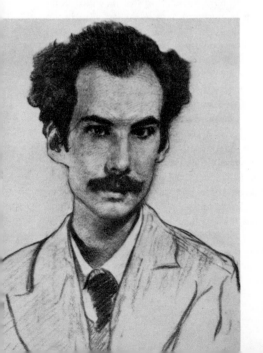

Lucifer as a Promethean rebel—beautiful as Christ and Apollo—protesting against injustice and tyranny. Since life itself is evil and man unhappy by nature, the greatest good would be the blessed calm of nothingness, the stillness of Nirvana. Combining Hindu and Buddhist religious philosophy with Schopenhauer's pessimism and misogyny, Strindberg's Lucifer—the bringer of light—regards sex and propagation as prolongations of human anguish and mercifully wishes to liberate humanity from the burden of existence. God has ceased to be the judge and has become the defendant, accused of a senseless and bungled act of creation. It is a grim irony that God's curses are life and love, and Lucifer's gifts death and annihilation.

The cosmic politics of *Coram Populo!* is played out in infinite space and unending time where a world devoid of meaning veers towards chaos and disaster. Strindberg's cataclysmic cosmogony, with its heretical vision of a usurper God and a deranged universe, anticipates the "cosmic cruelty" of Antonin Artaud and his short mystery, *The Spurt of Blood.*

*****

Pantomime is thinking overheard. It begins and ends before words have formed themselves, in a deeper consciousness than that of speech. . . . And pantomime has that mystery which is one of the requirements of true art. To watch it is like dreaming.

Arthur Symons

The symbolists wished to exclude distracting particularities of character and individual psychology from their dramas. Rather than the living human being, they extolled the depersonalized actor—puppet, marionette, and mask—as closer to the eternal. Pantomime exerted a special fascination, and no theatrical figure appealed more to the symbolist imagination than Pierrot, with his mask of flour, bereft of words, yet master of an eloquent language of silence. For poets, painters, and musicians in the last years of the nineteenth century, Pierrot was an artist and dreamer rejected by society who wore an ironic mask to conceal his wounded sensibility. This introspective, self-mocking Pierrot—a sad clown, a modern Hamlet at odds with the world—became a delicate register for the creative mind in the poetry of Verlaine and Laforgue, in the painting of Picasso and Ensor, in the songs of Schönberg. In the highly theatricalized life at the turn of the century, the cult of Pierrot had many votaries, none more bold than the young Russian actor and director Vsevolod Meyerhold, who identified with the role (which he played to perfection in Alexander Blok's *The Puppet Booth*) and had his portrait painted in the white costume and make-up of the *commedia* type.

The precursor of the Pierrot revival and creator of the first modern tragic Pierrot was Paul Margueritte. In 1881 during a summer vacation in the country, the twenty-one-year-old author wrote and acted *Pierrot, Assassin of His Wife*, improvising a stage out of boards and a trestle in an old barn loft. His uncle and next door neighbor, Stéphane Mallarmé, served as prompter, stage-manager, and producer and even wrote a prologue for the performance. It was *Pierrot, Assassin of His Wife* that led Mallarmé to formulate his theory of pantomime as a mirror of silence.

Possessed by his creation, who became his alter ego and double, Margueritte continued to present his pantomime for the next decade whenever and wherever he could—for friends and relatives, before peasants in rented ballrooms, in fashionable Parisian salons, and at special showings in professional theatres. For Margueritte, Pierrot was an archetype of the human soul, an embodiment of sacred horror, and a "tragic nightmare in the manner of . . . Edgar Poe." According to a critic of the time, Margueritte transformed the traditional *commedia* clown into "a sort of theatrical effigy of generalized humanity," like the protagonists in Greek tragedy; "his mouth, when he turns down the corners, resembled the copper embouchure of the mask of Orestes or of Agamemnon."

An artist in evil, Pierrot takes pleasure in the invention of sadistic crimes. And yet psychically Protean, the murderer becomes his own victim as he impersonates Colombine. By putting himself in her place, he undergoes the same agony. In the apocalyptic flames that engulf the bed, Pierrot falls prey to the fear that he has engendered; he is killed by his own imagination. Margueritte's interpretation of this dance of death was a virtuoso symbolist performance, achieved by his gliding enigmatically across the stage without a sound and freezing in statuesque poses with the rigidity of stone, all the while the ironic duplicity of his mask mysteriously inscrutable and his lunar pallor and the magic whiteness of his clothes expressive of the soul.

*****

Oh, if you only know how much silence we carry within ourselves.
Villiers de l'Isle-Adam

I see myself as an onlooker taking pleasure in silence.
Fernand Khnopff

The task of symbolist drama is to reveal the eternal behind the fleeting. Moments of sudden epiphany occur in silence, after the trite words of daily intercourse have fallen still. Artaud said of Maeterlinck that he was the first to introduce into literature "the multiple richness of the subconscious." With *The Intruder*, which launched symbolism in the theatre in 1891, Maeterlinck created an interior drama in which the mystery is revealed in a contemporary setting within the normal round of everyday life. An ordinary room with its human community is invaded by a stranger who—unlike the intruder in realistic social drama—brings not a temporal secret from this world, but an eternal secret from the other world. Henceforth invasion by an alien presence becomes an essential dramatic device in symbolist drama, and the progeny of *The Intruder* include the many visitors, wayfarers, and strangers who appear in turn-of-the-century plays.

In the Maeterlinckian drama of intrusion, structures of the soul replace those of society. Instead of economic groups and social classes, there are psychic differentiations determined by one's receptivity to the unknown and awareness that we are "playthings of the vast and heedless forces that surround us." Children and old people are most responsive to origins and endings. The pragmatic middle years become mired in the trivial facts of daily life, and those committed to the rational are inevitably blinded to the mystery of fatality and death. The banal conversation of the Uncle and Father in *The Intruder* as they try to ward off the menace of the unknown with their smug logic is of an absurdity worthy of Ionesco.

"Unhappiness must always remain the portion of man," Maeterlinck writes, "and the fatal abyss be ever open before him, vowed as he is to death, to the fickleness of matter, to old age and disease." His characters, "born without reason, to die," are not

Portrait of Madame Rachilde by Langlois

Portrait of Valerii Briusov
by Mikhail Vrubel'

Self-Portrait by Leonid Andreyev

autonomous individuals, but puppets and marionettes, victims of malevolent powers, to which they passively surrender. Their lack of purposefulness enraged the drama critics of the time, who in an age of progress and positivism could not tolerate a dramatic universe in which dreadful things happened arbitrarily to "poor little trembling creatures, who shivered for an instant and wept, on the brink of a gulf."

Introducing a minimalist art to the theatre, the Belgian playwright abolished traditional plot and reduced speech to stammerings and echoes. In order to dramatize the quiet, seemingly non-dramatic moments of life—"those meanings inhabiting silence and darkness . . . those inscrutable and intangible realities of the interior life"—Maeterlinck created a secret language, a dialogue of the second degree in which pauses and silences are weighted with significance and single words repeated like an incantation. The author of *The Intruder* praised Ibsen's *Master Builder* for its somnambulism, and his own short plays celebrate stasis. In Maeterlinck's new stagecraft, "the silence of doors and windows"—which in boulevard drama were only means of egress and ingress for lovers—become perspectives on eternity, points of access to a transcendent world. Behind the hypnotic and dream-like façade of Maeterlinck's plays, there lurks a muted violence at the eye of the hurricane. As Artaud pointed out, "We are at the very source of the tempest, in the circles immobile as life."

*****

We are the mirrors of the stellar light.

William Butler Yeats

The world is an immense Narcissus in the act of contemplating itself.

Joachim Gasquet

Now the image in the mirror was the stronger, and I was the mirror. I stared at that mysterious, terrifying stranger before me, and it seemed to me appalling to be alone with him.

Rainer Maria Rilke

The feminine Night is, like Thought, receptive, passive, immobile, contemplative, infinite, unformed and multiformed, in the same way as the Day is active, mobile, energetic, limited and finite.

Albert Samain

The symbolists were responsive to the structures of the year with its four seasons, to the diurnal cycle of light and dark, preferring these eternal rhythms to the contrivances of manipulated form. Favored by poets and musicians, in emulation of Chopin, nocturnes were symbolist hymns to the powers of darkness. The night is magical, dominated by the moon—source of Pierrot's pallor and madness—and conducive to dreams wherein man is freed from the historical order.

Rachilde's *Crystal Spider* is a lunar drama of the psyche obsessed with its own image, a nocturne devoted to the related symbolist motifs of mirror, moon, water, and spider. According to Gide in *The Treatise on Narcissus: Theory of the Symbol*, all of symbolism is contained in the myth of the beautiful youth who falls in love with his reflection in the pool. Separated from his own being, Narcissus yearns to unite with his twin self, but joining the image in the depths means a descent into the unconscious and and a loss of outer shape. Destruction lurks in the pool; the narcissus is the death flower. Such is the myth that serves as a subtext for Rachilde's play.

The moon is a reflecting pool luring the self-contemplator to his death. The mirror too is water immobilized; in its depths can be seen streaming hair and undulating forms (as in Gustav Klimt's "Fish Blood"). "Water is alive like a great silence in material form," writes Gaston Bachelard. It takes on the ever-changing shapes of destiny. The spider is a lunar creature, sitting at the center of the world, eternal spinner of the web of illusion. Like the moon, it holds sway over the phenomenal world and weaves the threads of each man's destiny. In certain myths, the moon is depicted as a giant spider.

Both male and female in their sexuality (*le miroir* and *la glace* in French), mirrors terrify the young hero of Rachilde's play—clad all in white with a pallid expressionless face like a sad Pierrot—because they afford frightening glimpses of other buried selves and disclose the unknown in all its seductive corruption. By removing social masks, the mirror ushers in doubles, and the terror-stricken victim is unable to flee from the demonic presences that haunt his childhood memories.

In the night consciousness of Rachilde's plays, novels, and tales, perverse sexuality occupies a central position, revealing a subterranean dream world of forbidden desire subversive of the social order. Admiringly called "Mademoiselle Baudelaire" and "Mademoiselle Salamander" by her peers, but considered by the police a pornographer for books like *Monsieur Venus* and *The Marquise de Sade* (in which male and female sexual roles are inverted), Rachilde violated taboos in her treatment of incest, bestiality, and deviant sexuality. Published in her collection of stories and plays, *The Demon of the Absurd*, *The Crystal Spider* dramatizes the destructive power of eros in its primordial and malevolent aspect.

*****

In this terrible hour only the dead are alive.

Fyodor Sologub

I do not differentiate life from dreaming nor from death, nor this world from the other world.

Alexander Blok

Set in the tower of the solitary self, Hofmannsthal's *Death and the Fool* is a lyrical drama of introspection, combining the theme of Narcissus and that of the Intruder. This monodrama probing a single consciousness takes the shape of a modern dance of death and summoning of Everyman, now a *fin-de-siècle* aesthete who views life as a dream until awakened from his reverie by the reality of man's mortality. The hero Claudio is an errant soul in search of a second self: in the form of a girl (like him in her disdain and disillusion) whom he has loved and abandoned, and of the friend whose thoughts and sweetheart he has shared and betrayed. With the exquisite *objets d'art* that surround him, he attempts an intimate communion, hoping to penetrate their inner natures. But he has refused to give himself to anyone or anything, living only for the moment in a voluptuous abandonment to every sensation. Such a Protean, dream-like existence in the world of fleeting appearances—despite its imaginative riches—leads to a sense of loneliness and isolation.

In *Death and the Fool*, passionate commitment to life brings Death—for the care-worn mother, broken-hearted girl, honor-bound friend. By insisting on his artistic sensibility with its multiplicity of selves, Claudio has escaped definition and survived them all. Yet his life is a death, and their death a life. Symbolist playwrights work endless variations on this central paradox, which will be taken up a generation later by the Expressionists in a social and political context, as witness the "death-in-life" and "life-in-death" of Ernst Toller's *Transfiguration.*

"Death, be my life!" Claudio cries out, succumbing to the temptation for union with another offered by the Intruder. This beautiful figure (who resembles a younger Claudio) is Eros-Thanatos, a Greek god of insinuating charm, not a medieval spectre of bone, cowl, and scythe. The Stranger is a vital erotic presence, akin to both Dionysus and Venus, an androgynous partner for all who join in the round dance of life and death. He has already seduced the Mother, Sweetheart, and Friend. As is indicated by the title in German (*Der Tor und Tod*), Death is Claudio's double—the other for whom the cool, detached aesthete has been yearning.

Dionysus, god of the instinctual and irrational, triumphs over the light-bearer Apollo, whose statue Claudio keeps in his garden. Nietzsche's *Birth of Tragedy* with its antithetical pair of terms, Dionysian and Apollonian, provides the dialectic for symbolist dramaturgy. The conflict in *Death and the Fool* is also played out among the four elements. Claudio's narcissistic sensibility, passively receptive to all impressions, is drawn toward water (seas, storms, streams, tears)—but he must return to earth, descend into the dark clay from which he came, into the primeval matter that precedes existence.

Symbolists end their plays not with a denouement—the eternal antinomies can never be resolved—but with a striking theatrical image blending sound, movement, color, and shape. Such is the final tableau of *Death and the Fool* in its synthesis of iconography, music, and dance. As dusk falls and darkness rises from the earth, we see through the window—which serves as a frame for the picture within the stage picture—Death as a wandering musician (the pictorial equivalent of a nineteenth-century woodcut) playing a folk melody on his violin and leading his lovers after him. Someone "resembling Claudio"—his other self—joins in the dance, at the moment of death integrated into the community of the eternally "living."

*****

The further we penetrate into the consciousness of man, the less struggle do we discover.

Maurice Maeterlinck

Rabindranath Tagore appears as a living embodiment of all the major symbolist aspirations in the arts. He was the representative of an ancient civilization whose culture was still whole, "where [in Yeats's words] poetry and religion are the same thing." Holy man, prophet, sage, and teacher, Tagore was an artist who transcended all genres and categories. Author of some fifty plays and composer of over two thousand songs in Bengali, Tagore was a total man of the theatre who directed and acted in his own works as well as being responsible for the music and dance. In his later years he became a powerful symbolist painter.

Rejecting the commercial Bengali theatre, Tagore created a lyrical drama of the imagination requiring only a bare stage and simple symbolic objects. "The danger of the

West," he wrote, "appears to me to consist in the spectator wishing his truth to be too concrete." He returned to the roots of drama, using as his models classical Sanskrit plays and native Bengali folk performances and performers. In all his works for the stage—which were often given in amateur productions and outdoor settings—Tagore combined music, song, dance, pantomime, and spectacle with poetry and legend. At the end of his career, he turned to dance-dramas and musical plays. In his songs folk melodies and Indian classical music are united with Western harmony.

Karna and Kunti is based on an episode in the ancient Sanskrit epic, *Mahabharata*, which, along with the *Ramayana*, is the prime source of Hindu mythology about men and gods. These legends have continued to furnish Indian dramatists with subjects, much as *The Iliad* and *The Odyssey* have served the same function in the West. From the immense epic with its complex tales of heroic warfare and intrigue, Tagore has chosen a brief moment of meeting and recognition between mother and son. Child of the sun deity abandoned at birth, Karna has been brought up by a charioteer and become the champion of the warrior clan of Kauravas, while Kunti is the mother of the five Pandavas, their longtime enemies.

Subtly detheatricalizing the event, Tagore transforms what could be a grand emotional scene into a quiet pause of melancholy reflection and mystery. In keeping with symbolist principles, Tagore prefers to avoid dramatic action and conflict and to listen instead to the music of the soul. At sunset, by the holy river, "where silence rests on the water," the voice of his mother leads Karna "back to some primal world of infancy lost in twilit consciousness," on the eve of the battle in which he knows that he will be defeated. The longed for reconciliation does not come to pass, nothing changes; the waiting has been in vain—a characteristic device of Tagore's dramaturgy. The futility of the struggle becomes apparent to the warrior, who is left with the "calm expectation of defeat and death."

*****

The seagulls flew with mournful cries over the anguish-covered plain.

Konstantin Bal'mont

In a magic way a sound can evoke an entire life in endless perspective, a color can become a concerto, and a visual impression can arouse terrifying orgies in the depths of the soul.

Stanisław Przybyszewski

Yeats argued for a theatre of masks in which rounded three-dimensional character would be eliminated in favor of pictorial flatness, "as in Byzantine painting, where there is no mass, nothing in relief." In tragic moments, character gives way to "chimeras that haunt the edge of trance" and the "mask from whose eyes the disembodied looks." By leaving out a dimension of reality—depth and roundness—playwrights and painters (Puvis de Chavannes, Klimt, Denis, Vrubel') moved symbolist art toward stylized simplification and decorative abstraction. Two-dimensionality evokes the timeless, the immanent, the numinous. The theatre grew painterly and plays became works of visual art. The dramatic artist like the painter used colors, shapes, and textures for compositional design rather than to attempt illusionistic fidelity to an outer reality. Bareness in staging and boldness in ornamental arrangement of form impart a sense of mythic space and time.

Closely allied in their goals, symbolist painters and playwrights by preference chose the statuesque pose, the suspended moment before dramatic action. Speaking of Michelangelo's figures, Gustave Moreau praises the "Beauty of Inertia" and declares that they "seem to be frozen in gestures of an ideal somnambulism." Instead of the confrontational and the histrionic, symbolist aesthetics prized ecstatic expectancy and hushed waiting—most often, for something that never comes to pass. At the greatest crises, movement becomes minimal; symbolist theatre slows to a point of excrutiatingly intense stillness. Retardation and slow motion replace the ever-accelerated pace found in the drama of external action. For Yeats the immobilization of life has the highest theatrical values: "the intensity of the trance," "life trembling into stillness and silence," and "the celebration of waiting."

The Shadowy Waters—a play that Yeats began writing early and worked on throughout much of his career—has the pictorial qualities and "vague enchanted beauty" (in T.S. Eliot's phrase) of a Pre-Raphaelite painting. "The whole picture as it were moves together—sky and sea and cloud are as it were actors," Yeats wrote; "The play is dreamy and dim and the colours should be the same—(say) a blue-green sail against an indigo-blue blackcloth, and the mast and bulwark indigo-blue. The persons in blue and green with some copper ornament." Appalled by the spiritual poverty of plays about the middle classes living in modern commercial cities, Yeats turned to the primitive imagination and savage folklore of the Irish past. The Shadowy Waters draws upon the Celtic Mysteries for the image of the journey of the self in its quest for immortality. The legendary voyager hero, Forgael—an Orphic figure with a magical harp—pursues a transcendent reality, and in his renunciation of earthly love for the Infinite, The Shadowy Waters is a version of Villiers de l'Isle-Adam's Axel (which the Irish poet saw in Paris in 1894). Wagnerian echoes come from both Tristan and Isolde and The Flying Dutchman, whose lovers—like Forgael and Dectora—sail beyond the boundaries of the phenomenal world to experience a lyrical liebestod.

Of The Shadowy Waters, Yeats declared, "It is almost religious; it is more a ritual than a human story. It is deliberately without human characters." The sea and its birds are dominant presences in a world ruled by primeval animism. In his Autobiography Yeats describes the origins of the play in the expeditions he made as a boy down to the sea at Sligo to hear the cry of the birds. Human-headed birds, embodying the souls of men, serve as pilots of the dream ship on which Forgael and Dectora escape the confines of reality for eternity. For Yeats, the flight of birds is "an expression of the Anima Mundi as is the artist's creation of images."

*****

> But a threatening Shadow follows me everywhere,
> and I do not know when I shall be freed
> from this darkness—by God's deliverance.
>
> Tadeusz Miciński

The dramatic epilogue Visitors—the last in a series of four plays collectively titled Love's Dance of Death—is the theatrical counterpart of a painting by Przybyszewski's friend Edvard Munch. In works such as The Dance of Life and Death and Ashes, Munch conveys

"Death and the Fool"
by Angelo Jank (1899).

Meyerhold as Pierrot
by Nikolai Yul'yanov (1908)

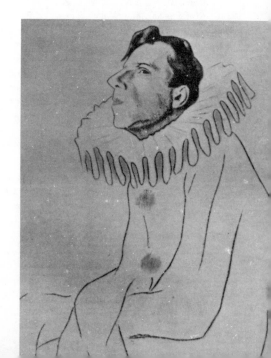

Drawing of a Head
by Jeanne Jacquemin (1894)

feelings of anxiety, the menace of sexuality, and the ultimate horror of life. A perceptive critic of the Norwegian artist, Przybyszewski declared that Munch's goal was "to express, in fine, the naked psychological state, not mythologically, that is, by means of sensory metaphors, but direcly in its coloristic equivalent." *Visitors* is a comparable rendering of the demonic world of psychic phenomena through a painterly use of stark lines, raw colors, and dark engulfing shadows.

Munch depicted Przybyszewski several times. In *Portrait of Stanisław Przybyszewski*, the Polish writer stares blankly ahead, eyes deranged, cigarette dangling from his mouth, and in *Jealousy*, the same head appears at one side of the canvas, gazing out fixedly—while perceiving in an inner vision the figures of Adam and Eve who stand behind him to his left. During his "Inferno crisis," Strindberg felt that he was pursued by the Satanic Przybyszewski who remained invisible behind a wall of greenery playing Schumann's *Aufschwung*. The author of *Visitors* was, in fact, a brilliant interpreter of Chopin who would sit at the piano (on which there always stood a glass of rum) and play the nocturnes as if in a trance. Przybyszewski calls for the playing of Saint-Saens's *Danse macabre* throughout *Visitors*, but it could be just as well Schumann or Chopin, interpreted by the playwright himself who almost seems to be present in his own drama—in the lower right hand corner of the stage frame, wild-eyed and demented, a cigarette between his lips. Behind him, Adam, Bela, and Pola are figures in his mind's eye, projections of his psyche. Przybyszewski is the play's dreamer; it is a theatre of "the naked soul."

Visitors takes the form of a dance of death in which all humanity is driven by relentless urges in a desperate masquerade. As in Poe's *Masque of the Red Death* and Ensor's paintings, the dead and the dying are celebrants at a masqued ball in carnival time. Przybyszewski's "Haunted Palace"—inspired by Poe—is the habitation of the soul, image of a mind peopled by phantoms, the architecture of a disordered brain. In his evocation of primal desire and pyschic terror, Przybyszewski calls upon Aztec rites of sun worship, tales of vampires with frightful black wings, and the paranoia of the persecuting double. *Visitors* is a descent into the vortex of madness from which the only escape is suicide; the mansion dissolves into darkness, much as the House of Usher sinks into the earth.

Within the divided psyche lurks the other self—hidden and unknown—that punishes with guilt for uncommitted crimes. Using the themes of double and shadow, which were often combined in nineteenth-century fantastic literature, Przybyszewski conceives of Adam's shadow as an astral double that has become detached from his body—only to reappear as the moment of death draws near. At the same time that Freud was formulating his theory of the subconscious in *The Interpretation of Dreams*, the author of *Visitors* maintained that "Sexuality is the primal substance of life" and presented the metaphysics of love as a savage battle between the sexes. The world of eros has been infected by an evil spirit. "Nature is wicked, fiendish, lying, crafty," writes Przybyszewski. Laughter in *Visitors* is spasmodic and hollow, the outcry of an anguished demon. A proponent of heretical gnosticism well versed in satanism and infernal rites, Przybyszewski conceived of a church for those like Adam (both the character in *Visitors* and his great ancestor) who are cursed and in despair; the playwright's disciples in Cracow banded together and called themselves the "Sons of Satan."

*****

The sense of mystery lies in always being in the equivocal, in double and triple aspects.

Odilon Redon

The stage that is in the poet's mind has no lack of space or appurtenance.

Rabindranath Tagore

The past of the Celtic race was the great storehouse of myth and legend for the symbolists. Wagner showed the way with *The Flying Dutchman, Tristan and Isolde,* and *Parsifal,* and Maeterlinck followed with *The Death of Tintagiles* and *Pelléas and Mélisande.* Yeats and Synge revived ancient Irish mythology, and the painters Emile Bernard and Paul Gauguin went to the Celtic roots of the old culture of Brittany in their quest for Breton folklore. In the same spirit of the Spanish poet, playwright, and novelist Ramon del Valle-Inclán turned to his native Galicia and found in the legends and superstitions of this archaic province a rich source of Celtic atavism. Fascinated by the magical and the primitive (he wrote a series of "barbaric comedies"), the Spanish author explored the fabulous in the murky past of the region and collected folk beliefs and practices, taking delight in bizarre accounts of sorcery, demonic possession, and curses and spells.

Blurring distinctions between narrative and dramatic, story and play, Valle-Inclán places *The Dream Comedy* in *A Shadowy Garden,* a collection of fantastic stories about saints, souls in torments, elves and thieves, purportedly told by an aged servant of the author's grandmother to the young boy. These tales full of tragic and naive mystery terrified the writer during his childhood years; now they come back to haunt his memory. "And as if a cold and silent wind had passed over them, they give off the long murmur of dead leaves. The murmur of an old abandoned garden!" In the iconography of symbolism, deserted parks and gardens are the special refuge for dreamers.

The Dream Comedy is a tale of enchantment and obsession that spills out beyond the frame of the stage. Stretching the dimensions of traditional scenic space, Valle-Inclán uses cinematographic techniques that seem to defy the resources of the theatre and challenge its resources. In all his plays, the Spanish writer provides extensive stage directions (sometimes in rhymed verse) that evoke a cruel and sensual world of the imagination which the director must match by his own powers of invention. The brigand captain in *The Dream Comedy* continues his pursuit of the severed hand for all eternity as he chases after but can never overtake the spectral dog who has escaped with the holy relic between his teeth. Dramatic closure is denied as the sound of galloping hooves echoes on and on. The primitive animism of the hand that acquires a life of its own after having been cut off by a single blow of the Captain's sabre anticipates an episode in *The Andalusian Dog*—by Valle-Inclán's fellow countrymen Buñuel and Dali—where a severed hand lying in the street is prodded by an androgynous girl and put in a box by a policeman. In his creation of a grotesque and dream-like language of images, Valle-Inclán prepares the way for Spanish Surrealism.

*****

People are ghosts playing at being people.

Konstantin Somov

It is the most elementary philosophical thought that there is no border between reality and revery, between life and death.

Valerii Briusov

Alexander Blok's plays belong to the phase of Russian symbolism in which the mockery of disbelief attacks the ideal. All that the author holds sacred is subjected to diabolical laughter and sinister doubling. The adored Beautiful Lady of Blok's youthful poems turns into a whore; the falling star becomes a fallen woman. "I am fated to experience the Babylonian harlot," the poet confesses. Transcendental—or metaphysical—irony, as Blok defines it, underlines the artificiality and absurdity of everyday life seen from the perspective of eternal tragedy. When man becomes an inauthentic puppet or plaything made of cardboard, laughter from the demon of banality can be heard.

Classified by Blok as a lyrical drama, *The Stranger* takes the form of a triptych with three visions—of tavern, street, and salon—instead of scenes. A single consciousness holds sway through which reality is refracted, giving rise to kaleidoscopic transformations. In the preface to three *Lyrical Dramas*, Blok discloses that his characters are "different sides of the soul of one man" and that "they all seek a beautiful, free, bright life, which alone can lift from their weak shoulders the burden—beyond their strength—of doubt and contradictions and drive away importunate and spectral doubles."

Unity of personality disintegrates, and doubles proliferate. The first and third visions—the low-life tavern and the fashionable salon—are mirror images. Forever splitting in two (as does the scenery, revealing new settings), the Stranger is half star, half woman, embodying both the ideal of the Madonna and the ideal of Sodom. The Poet's persona divides into Azure, his spiritual alter ego, and the Astrologer, his earthly anti-face; all three find an antipodal double in the Gentlemen in the Derby, a cynical man about town, who plays the role of Harlequin to the Poet's Pierrot and the Stranger's Colombine (the *commedia* triangle in Blok's earlier play, *The Puppet Show*).

As the two epigraphs from *The Idiot* indicate, the Stranger is also a double of the holy sinner, Nastasia Filipovna, who tortures herself and her masochistic lovers in Dostoevsky's novel. The dramatic version of *The Stranger* (like the poem of the same name that preceded it) takes place in a Dostoevskian urban landscape, and we can find on a map precisely where the tavern of the first vision is located (not far from where Svidrigailov in *Crime and Punishment* committed suicide). Blok is a poet of the nighttime streets of St. Petersburg, exemplar of the "tentacular cities" celebrated by the Belgian symbolist Emile Verhaeren and his Russian followers. *The Stranger* is a descent into the nocturnal labyrinth of the great modern metropolis and an exploration of its eroticism. "Is there beauty in Sodom?" asks Dmitri in *The Brothers Karamazov*, "God and the devil are fighting there and the battlefield is in the heart of man." The apocalyptic symbol of the Virgin—object of the gnostic cult of Sophia (Wisdom) preached by the philosopher Vladimir Solovyov—has been debased and trampled in the mud. The play was at first forbidden by the censor because of its blasphemous allusions to Mary.

Circularity and endless repetition characterize the fallen world of *The Stranger* with its echoing, trivializing dialogue. During the exceptionally snowy winter of 1906-1907, Blok had been reading *The Birth of Tragedy*, as well as rereading Dostoevsky, and the Nietzschean concept of Eternal Recurrence informs the play. The idea that every event in the universe must recur an infinite number of times in exactly the same way is a cause of dread, generating horror at the aimlessness of existence and the senselessness of time. The mindless ritual of society—whether in tavern or salon—is a closed circle. In his productions of Blok's plays, Meyerhold took this ceremonial side of life, the masquerade of marionettes, and created a grotesque "theatre of social masks."

Like Picasso and other painters at the turn of the century, Blok makes use of color as a dominant element to define the mood of *The Stranger* and convey its dreamlike quality. Blue plays a crucial role in symbolist aesthetics; it was the modernist color par excellence. Goethe had said of blue that it "arouses anxiety and nostalgia." For the *fin de siècle*, it was the color of art and artists, of dreams and dreamers. *The Stranger* is composed and unified through different tonalities of blue and azure set against the darkness of the night. In the works of Baudelaire and Mallarmé, azure defines the sphere of beauty and the limitless world of the ideal. The Stranger is, in Blok's words, "a diabolic fusion of blue and lilac," similar to Vrubel's demon—a star fallen to earth—fiery and radiant—in the encroaching blackness.

*****

Those same feelings which the whole of Europe had experienced around the year 1000 A.D., when it expected the end of the World and the Last Judgment, were relived in the circle of young Moscow mystics. But the fateful time came and went and their prophecies had not come true. A period of disillusion and disbelief followed, which led them at times to mock what they had once held sacred.

Valerii Bruisov

As the Tsarist Empire began to crumble and the first tremors made themselves felt in the unsuccessful revolution of 1905, apocalypse seemed immanent in contemporary history, and the Book of Revelation became the basic text of the times. Whereas the coming End of the World is largely a poetic figure of speech in the West, in Russia eschatological thinking was a national phenomenon. Overwhelmed by a sense of impending catastrophe, preachers of the final judgment rose up in all classes of Russian society.

Waiting for the Antichrist became the subject of a number of apocalyptic dramas at the *fin de siècle*, and in the works of Andrei Bely, the "sensation of the abyss" was particularly pronounced. Dread, doubt, and satanic laughter subvert joyous anticipation of the Second Coming. Before the glow of a new dawn comes the glacial darkness ushered in by the reign of the Antichrist, the appearance of false messiahs, and the return to primordial chaos. The historical crisis enters the demonic phase.

Jaws of Night is a drama of eschatological premonitions, played out in murky interstellar space and indeterminate time. Since the sun has been extinguished and all entities subjected to the power of negation, night and day are no longer distinguishable. Caught between two epochs at the point where past and future intersect, symbolist playwrights create dualistically—from antithetical pairs of terms, such as Christ and Antichrist, light and dark, heights and depths—and strive for a unity of polar opposites. What the fifteenth-century mystic, churchman, philosopher, mathematician, and political theorist, Nicholas of Cusa, called *coincidentia oppositorum* (or union of contraries in God) become the essential technique of Bely and his fellow dramatists, whereby the mystery of totality is affirmed and "ultimate reality is defined by pairs of opposites" (in the words of Mircea Eliade).

Sharing Heraclitus's notion that all things carry within them their own opposite, Bely in his Antichrist plays penetrates to the primordial state in which contraries exist as complementary aspects of a single reality; cosmos and chaos, creation and destruction, Christ and Antichrist are perceived as inseparably linked. In *Notes of an Eccentric*, the author of *Jaws of Night* locates the source of his Antichrist plays in a vision he saw in

Portrait of Stanisław Przybyszewski
by Edvard Munch (1898)

"Sun Sonata" (Allegro)
by Mikalojus K. Čiurlionis (1907)

Paul Margueritte as Pierrot

church during Holy Week. "It was as if one wall of the church opened into the void. I saw the End (I don't know of what—my life or the world's), but it was as if the road of history rested upon two domes—upon a Temple; and crowds of people thronged toward it. To myself, I called the Temple I saw the Temple of Glory and it seemed to me that Antichrist was threatening this Temple. I ran out of the church like a madman. . . . In the evening in my little room, I drafted the plan for a mystery drama."

In *Jaws of Night*, Bely creates a landscape of the mind, he gives the soul its own topography, he assigns appropriate climate to spiritual states—and weather to the psyche. It is a symphony of sounds, a theatrical synthesis of light, color, movement, and shape, that draws inspiration from Arnold Böcklin's famous painting *The Isle of the Dead*, of which the Russian poet wrote: "We are struck by the correspondence among the human figure (enclosed in a white robe), the cliffs, the cypresses and the dark, gloomy sky."

Bely was one of the "Scythians," a mystical religious group who believed that Russia was the Messiah destined to usher in the culture of eternity. They welcomed the Bolshevik revolution as a "purifying power of destructive cataclysm." In the wave of material annihilation that would follow, a new period of primitive Christianity could arise when the persecuted church would shine brightly with a mysterious light. *Jaws of Night* forecasts the mood of ardent belief and fearful doubt called forth by visions of a disintegrating world during the cataclysmic years 1917-1920.

*****

The crowd of spectators must fuse into a choral body, like the mystical community of ancient "orgies" and "mysteries."

Vyacheslav Ivanov

I felt the feelings of the world mystically, with my mouth sealed by the seven hermetic seals, and my soul, imprisoned in the mire, trembled with the anguish of being mute.

Ramon del Valle-Inclán

Like his fellow symbolists, Miciński proposed a theatre temple in which the audience would participate as celebrants in a sacred rite. He envisaged a huge outdoor stage in the Tatras Mountains—which he identified with the Himalayas as the source of Indo-European man. Stanisław Wyspiański dreamed of an open air ampitheatre on the royal hill of Wawel (near Cracow), which would be like Bayreuth, but with three-dimensional decor. Yeats sought to establish an Irish equivalent of the Eleusian mysteries, or theatre of Dionysus, in an unoccupied castle of heroes. D'Annunzio planned a theatre of Apollo high up in Albano that would dominate the province of Campania. The Russian composer Scriabin conceived a grandiose outdoor theatre to be built in India with the Himalayas serving as background. An audience of thousands was to sit in a semicircle, reflected in a vast pool of water. Sunrises and sunsets would become part of the stage decor, and bells were to be suspended from the clouds over the mountains. The performance—a union of music, dance, and song—would last for seven days; at the end of the twelfth hour of the seventh day, a new race of humankind would be born, combining male and female, and the world would come to an end in a triumphal conflagration.

Although none of these projects could ever be realized, in *The Ballad of the Seven Sleeping Brothers in China* Miciński attempts to unite the spectators in the theatre with the audience of madmen watching the play within a play created by the Poet. The drama takes place in a harshly modern world: in a rundown asylum for the insane, distraught patients are abused by overworked doctors who regard the mentally ill as hopeless cases and beaten by sadistic guards who inject them with numbing drugs. The Poet-Madman recounts a mystical journey to the East that becomes a performance, a ritual enactment of the plight of the listeners. A huge mirror dominates the house in the Hindu style where the Sleeping Brothers are found, and the Chinese Princess holds a smaller looking glass in her hand. The tale of spiritual transformation told by the poet mirrors the closed world of the asylum; it is a story about the group itself, designed to arouse the ludic impulse and awaken the sleepers through the liberating wisdom of the East.

The deranged sit in a semi-circle extending outwards to encompass the auditorium. All madmen are invited to participate as the grim routine of the madhouse is transmuted into the celebration of a sacred rite. The dreary chronological time of endless incarceration is inscribed in the mythic time of an eternal realm. By means of a dramatic technique of radical disorientation, that never explains, anticipates nothing, and leads nowhere, Miciński creates the sense of a "continuous present" that Gertrude Stein felt should be the special province of theatre. Lack of internal plot connections makes it impossible to regard past or future; there is only pure duration, the moment being lived, the sensation of existence. As in Poe's *Eureka*, "Space and Duration are one . . . neither Past nor Future . . . all being Now."

The mythic subsoil of Miciński's *Ballad* is the legend of the Seven Sleepers (Christian youths of Ephesus who, fleeing Roman persecution, slept in a cave for 230 years), which according to Philippe Aries is a parable of waiting for the Day of Judgment. Its mystic number evokes other symbolist works, such as Maeterlinck's *Seven Sleeping Princesses*, Bartok and Balázs's *Bluebeard* with its seven wives and seven doors, and Khnopff's *Memories* which replicates seven images of the artist's sister as a British croquet player. As with the Sleeping Knights in Burne-Jones's *Briar Rose* cycle, the mute world of frozen time—peopled with crumbling corpses—imparts a heightened theatricality to the Poet's mysterious narrative. Somnolence and sleep-walking lie at the heart of symbolist aesthetics.

In Miciński's *Ballad*, three worlds—the brightly colored dreams of the insane, the sterile confinement of the asylum, and the cold, distant cosmos—intersect, but cannot interact. Their lines cross in the brain of the Poet-Madman, who, like Vrubel's Demon, in his anguished vision of human suffering has a more profound form of consciousness than the sane. He is microcosmic man; what takes place in his individual psyche is expressive of the universe. When he hangs himself with his strait jacket, a dying meteor glows vastly in the sky.

*****

I believe only in what I do not see.

Gustave Moreau

The poet is the priest of the invisible.

Wallace Stevens

Valerii Briusov, chief spokesman for Russian symbolism, attended seances in Moscow, contributed to the spiritualist journal *Rebus*, and showed passionate interest in medieval witchcraft, black magic, and occultism, doing extensive research for his novel about demonic possession, *The Fiery Angel*. In 1892 Briusov translated Maeterlinck's *Intruder*, and he saw a production of the play at a private club in Moscow in 1900. In a poem entitled "The Intruder," he portrays himself as a corpse in the embraces of his beloved: "In your arms I shall be dead the whole night through." In a series of erotic ballads, the Russian poet works variations on Baudelaire's comparison of lovers to dead bodies and delves into Poe's necrophilia. Briusov had the knack of entering into perverse psychic states; he could exoticize the everyday and render convincing morbid sexual fantasies. Inspired by a sixteenth-century German woodcut by Nicolas Deutsch, he wrote "Das Weib und Der Tod," in which the Maiden, admiring herself in a mirror, suddenly catches sight of Death—the unexpected visitor—who kisses her on the lips, rudely tips her over, and lifts up her skirt.

In *The Wayfarer*, which Briusov calls a "psychodrama," the playwright fuses *The Intruder* with the medieval motif of "Death and the Maiden" (much favored by symbolist painters such as Munch, Ensor, and Kubin). Yet at the same time the heroine Julia is portrayed realistically, with precise social and psychological notation, like one of Chekhov's dissatisfied provincial women, bored with the uneventfulness of life and dreaming of going to the capital. Briusov believed that symbolism should seek new material in the contemporary world. "The poet, always like Antaeus, gains his strength only *from contact with the earth*," he wrote; "The basis of all art is the observation of reality."

> We live in the world of the telegraph, the telephone, the stock-exchange, the theatre, the scientific congress, the world of ocean liners and express trains, but poets continue to use images which are completely alien to us, which are preserved only in verse, images which turn the world of poetry into a dead and conventionalized world.

If the subject of *The Wayfarer* is Chekhovian, the mode is symbolist: to call into question the objectivity of external reality by probing human consciousness and the mechanism of perception. "Realism is the means, and not the end of art," Briusov declared. The drama of *The Wayfarer* is internalized within the mind of the dreamer. The play is a seance at which Julia invokes the presence of the Wayfarer and creates imaginary lives for him and for herself, enacting the fairy tale of the Stranger-Prince. Gripped by desire to unite with another, Julia attempts to define the other first through her fears, then through her longings. She discovers her unknown self in the mirror of the Wayfarer, in the voice of his silence. An excursion in the poetry of loneliness, *The Wayfarer* dramatizes a desperate effort to know something other than the self and to break out of intolerable human isolation.

In 1902 Briusov attacked realism as practiced by the Moscow Art Theatre, rejecting the idea that real life could be shown on stage. Instead Briusov argued, "We should grasp the unearthly (the supernatural, the mysterious) through local symbols of the here and now." As an art with its own language of sounds, colors, and shapes, theatre is a system of expressive signs superior to any attempts at achieving direct correspondence with reality. In an essay on "Realism and Convention" (1908), Briusov maintains a strikingly modern position: since the living human being prevents any complete stylization in the theatre, performance must rely on the actor's body on an open, uncluttered stage as its principal resource. Asserting that "the only purpose of the theatre is to assist the actor to reveal his soul before the spectators," the leader of the Russian symbolists advances a daring and radical position, challenging the traditional view that performance should serve and illuminate the playwright's text. "Artistic, aesthetic enjoyment in the theatre we receive from the performers, and not from the play," he claims; "The author is the servant of the actors."

Briusov, who served as Meyerhold's literary advisor at the Theatre Studio and was the theoretician for the director's new stage language (as revealed in the production of Maeterlinck's *Death of Tintagiles*), created *The Wayfarer* as a monodrama for an actress. The performer, like the lyric poet, speaks directly to the audience. In her solitude and anguish, Julia addresses the spectators and tries to enlist their aid. For her, there is "no fixed boundary between the real world, between 'dreaming' and 'waking,' 'life' and 'fantasy.'" She has penetrated deeper and deeper into the kingdom of her visions and taken the audience with her on the journey.

*****

> *Simplicity in him, being the most laughable thing in the world, [Pierrot] becomes learned, perverse, intellectualising his pleasure, brutalising his intellect; his mournful contemplation of things becoming a kind of grotesque joy.*
>
> Arthur Symons

> *In the theatre of the future there will be no spectators. People will act for themselves, without audiences and actors, by themselves.*
>
> Leonid Andreyev

> *Pierrot has the moon mania of a hysterical artist of today, he has his vibrating susceptibility for Chopin's music and for tormenting thoughts, for the sound of the violin, for gaudy red and for "holy" soft white.*
>
> Hugo von Hofmannsthal

Pierrot and the world of *commedia* provided the symbolist imagination with a means of exploring its own resources and inner workings. Wallace Stevens's monodrama, *Carlos Among the Candles*, is a communion of the poetic consciousness with its own perceptions—conducted by a Pedant-Pierrot obsessed with creative naming. Like Claudio in Hofmannsthal's *Death and the Fool*, Stevens's hero (one of the poet's many versions of Pierrot) carries on an intense dialogue with things. In a letter of 1916, Stevens declared, "The play is simply intended to demonstrate that just as objects in nature offset us . . . so, on the other hand, we affect objects in nature, by projecting our moods, emotions, etc.," and in 1935 he commented that "it has to do with the effect of changing light on the emotions."

Amid flickering candles, the dreaming soul is attracted to night thoughts. A nocturne on the interplay of subject and object, *Carlos Among the Candles* plays upon symbolist themes of metamorphosis, instability of natural forms, and merging of animate and inanimate. Beyond the window is a vast and alien universe; Carlos is threatened by the "despairing darkness" outside. The room of the mind must undergo "Domination of Black"—the title of a poem by Stevens about fear and isolation felt upon the coming of night. A midnight colloquy with the self, *Carlos Among the Candles* is a companion piece

Illustration for Briusov's "In the Mirror" by Alberto Martini (1910)

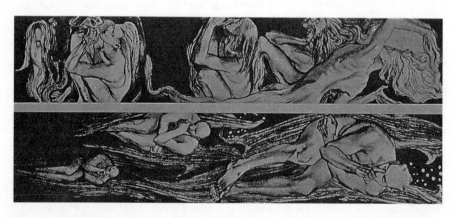

"Fire and Air" from The Four Elements by Stanisław Wyspiański (1897)

to Mallarmé's *Igitur*, where at twelve, in a claustral room with drawn curtains, the poet—illumined by a single candle that he soon blows out—confronts consciousness in the void (although Stevens could not have known Mallarmé's work, which was not published until 1924).

Carlos, who first enters on stage with a bound, leaves by springing through the window out into the night "as blue as water"—the color of the imagination. His final leap of "grotesque joy" becomes a plunge into experience of what lies beyond in the larger void. It is like Narcissus's leap into the pool of water that is his mirror, or Pierrot's headlong plunge out of the window in Blok's *Puppet Show*. The window becomes the picture within the picture, an inner frame through which we look out (structurally similar to our view of Death and his dancers at the end of Hofmannsthal's *Death and the Fool*).

A critic of the time described *Carlos Among the Candles* as "not unlike a combination of Gertrude Stein's 'In a Department Store' and Henry James's story, 'The Altar of the Dead.' " Responding to uncomprehending reactions, Stevens mused, "A theatre without action or characters ought to be within the range of human interests." In its concern with pure perception—the refraction of color, light, sound—Stevens's monodrama shows affinities to the optical and auditory experiments of impressionist painters and musicians, of whom Renoir and Debussy are mentioned in the play. In its linguistic emphases—on the theurgic ability of the poet as creator of reality—*Carlos Among the Candles* bears out Briusov's assertion: "Great is the mystery of words and their power."

*****

Black must be respected. Nothing adulterates it. It does not give pleasure to the eye and awakens no sensuality. It is an agent of the mind far more than the fine color of the palette or prism.

Odilon Redon

Blocks of wood instead of people in the auditorium, and people portraying blocks of wood on stage.

Alexander Blok

The Prince of this world . . . who is he? The executioner to whom we have been delivered for crimes unknown or forgotten, which we have committed in another world!

August Strindberg

Planned by Andreyev as his swan song, an artistic and ideological last will and testament, *Requiem* is a midnight colloquy with the self in a closed space with no window on the beyond. The mood is reflexive and self-devouring. Theatre is a dungeon of the mind, and the dreamer is stifled, facing the terror of immured thought. The ludic impulse has gone sour; that commonplace of the European tradition—"all the world is a stage"—has become a sinister joke. The Great World, extolled by Hofmannsthal, has shrunk to a claustrophobic windowless enclosure (like one of Poe's dream chambers). The audience is included in the performance, but the celebrants are wooden dummies. The theatrical rites are now meaningless, the same gestures repeated endlessly and the old roles replayed again and again.

The House of the Dead, peopled with memories and specters, is an empty theatre—a later version of the Maeterlinckian castle with its heavy, clanging doors and labyrinthian passageways, hermetically sealed from the outside world. *Requiem* is a perverted cosmogony, in the ironic manner of Strindbrg's *Coram Populo!*, transposed into theatrical terms. The earth is a grim prison created by the Masked Prince of Darkness, who is the producer of the "show." "Let there be light" is reduced to bringing up the lights on stage, the creation of man to the entrance of a few puppets. *Requiem* calls attention to its own artificiality, bares its own devices—it is a corrosive work of auto-demolition reducing the dramatic event to paralysis and derision.

Andreyev's play is an example of what the contemporary German writer, Tankred Dorst, calls "drama of negation," which stresses the indeterminacy of the stage world and thus reflects a parallel uncertainty of values, morals, social norms in the world of the spectator. Combining "absolute appearance and simulated postures," drama of negation engenders tensions incapable of resolution. Northrop Frye classifies Andreyev's dramas as anti-masques, satyr plays or demonic moralities, taking place in a sinister limbo, in which characterization breaks down into dissociative elements of the personality. Andreyev argued that, since film can present external action more effectively, theatre must concentrate on the drama of thought and its inner struggles.

In creating the Man in the Mask, the playwright recalled the mysterious visitor who called on Mozart and commissioned him to write a Requiem that was soon to become the dying composer's own. Andreyev would have known a version of this legend in Pushkin's *Mozart and Salieri*. Goya's *Caprichos* (much admired by the symbolists) were also a source of inspiration for *Requiem* which shares their irrationality, ambiguity of setting, chiaroscuro lighting effects, and enigmatic characters in an uncanny, unknowable world. Andreyev, himself a painter, was equally devoted to the Russian popular arts, especially graphics depicting Petrushka, the native Pierrot and quintessential puppet of the fairground booths.

Composed during the devastations of World War I and the crumbling of the Tsarist Empire, *Requiem* is a dirge for a dying civilization, a burial rite for an exhausted theatrical tradition, as well as a deathwatch of the soul awaiting final dissolution. Although it gives a foretaste of Pirandello's theatre-in-the-theatre, Andreyev's *theatrum mundi* is poised over the abyss within a single consciousness. In the deserted house of the author's brain, behind its impenetrable walls, a midnight drama of disintegrating thought is played out in a private theatre of the mind, with ghosts as actors and grotesquely painted wooden dummies as audience. Andreyev makes a striking theatrical use of the dramatis personae as puppets-manikins-marionettes, a concept that has fascinated avant-gardists from Maeterlinck and Gordon Craig to Tadeusz Kantor. For in *Requiem* no living characters are in search of an author, but the creator himself is at an impasse, playing a desperate end game with the dead voices of the past. Variations on nothing, Andreyev's *Requiem* can be read as a Beckettian meditation on human isolation and loneliness, on the futility of human aspirations in a blank universe in which man is condemned to death.

*****

These plays are windows on the night, unexpected confrontations with existence, moments of cosmic horror in face of the void, questionings of a silent universe without shape or value in which the only truth is what the self creates. Starting with a mystery and ending with a requiem, the collection also has a place for dramas of apocalyptic expectancy, prognostic of social change and revolution—yet permeated with self-mocking disenchantment at the failure of the ideal to materialize. And everywhere there is a substratum of myth treated idiosyncratically rather than according to an already known system of recognizable signs. The symbolists preferred to synthesize diverse religious and mythological sources in a purely personal manner, rejecting the clarity and consistency of allegory for a musical blending of themes, whereby contradictory meanings are allow-ed to co-exist.

Coram Populo!

**De Creatione
Et Sententia
Vera Mundi**

A Mystery

August Strindberg

CHARACTERS:

The Eternal One, invisible.
God, the evil Spirit, usurper, the Prince of this world.
Lucifer, the Bearer of light, dethroned.
Archangels
Angels
Adam and Eve

Swedish version written and published 1878
French version published 1898
Translated from the French text in *Inferno* by Daniel Gerould

ACT I

Heaven

God and Lucifer, each on his throne. They are surrounded by angels. God is an old man with a severe, almost wicked countenance; he has a long white beard, and small horns like the Moses of Michelangelo.

Lucifer is young and beautiful, with something about him of Prometheus, Apollo, and Christ; his complexion is white and luminous, his eyes blaze, his teeth are white. There is a halo around his head.

GOD: Let there be movement, since repose has corrupted us! I wish to hazard one more manifestation, at the risk of squandering my strength and losing myself in the brutish multitude.

Look! Over there between Mars and Venus several megameters of my realm still remain unoccupied. There I wish to create a new world: from Nothingness it will be born, and to Nothingness it will one day return. The creatures who live there will believe themselves gods like ourselves, and it will be our pleasure to watch their struggles and their vanities. Let its name be the world of madness! What says my brother Lucifer who shares with me these realms in the Southern Milky Way?

LUCIFER: Lord, brother, thy evil will exacts suffering and misfortune. I execrate thy thought.

GOD: What say the Angels to my plan?

ANGELS: The Lord's will be done!

GOD: So be it! And woe unto them that enlighten the madmen as to their origin and destiny!

LUCIFER: Woe unto them that call evil good and good evil; that put darkness for light and light for darkness, that put bitter for sweet and sweet for bitter! I summon thee to the tribunal of the Eternal.

GOD: Well, I am waiting! For, dost thou meet the Eternal more than once every ten myriad of years when he visits these regions?

LUCIFER: I shall go tell the truth to mankind that thy schemes be annihilated.

GOD: Cursed be thou, Lucifer. And may thy place be found beneath the world of madness, so that thou seest their torments; and that mankind call thee the Evil one!

LUCIFER: Thou shalt conquer since thou art strong as Evil! For mankind thou shalt be God, thou, Satan, the calumniator!

GOD: Down with the rebel! Forward: Michael, Raphael, Gabriel, Uriel! Strike: Samael, Azarel, Mehazael! Blow: Oriens, Paymon, Egyn, Amaimon!

(Lucifer is carried off by a whirlwind and cast into the abyss.)

ACT II

On Earth

Adam and Eve under the Tree of Knowledge, then Lucifer in the form of a serpent.

EVE: I had not noticed that tree.

ADAM: That tree is forbidden us.

EVE: Who has said so?

ADAM: God!

LUCIFER: (Entering.) Which God? There are many!

ADAM: Who is speaking?

LUCIFER: I, Lucifer, the Bearer of light, who desires your happiness, who suffers your sufferings. Look at the new star of morning that announces the return of the sun! That is my star, surmounted by a mirror that reflects the light of the Truth. Its rays, in the fullness of time, will guide certain shepherds in a certain desert towards a manger where will be born my son, the redeemer of the world.

   As for that tree, as soon as you have eaten of it you will know good and evil. You will then know that life is evil; that you are not gods, that the Evil One has struck you blind, and that your existence unfolds only to serve as a laughingstock for the gods. Eat of it and you will possess the gift of deliverance from sorrows, the joy of death!

EVE: I desire to know and to be delivered! Eat of it also, Adam!

(They eat the forbidden fruit.)

ACT III

Heaven

God and Uriel.

URIEL: Woe unto us, since our joy is ended.
GOD: What has happened?
URIEL: Lucifer has revealed your actions to the inhabitants of the earth; they know all and are happy.
GOD: Happy! Woe unto them! . . .
URIEL: What is more, he has given them the gift of liberty, so that they can return to nothingness.
GOD: By dying! Good! Let them propagate before they die. Let there be love!

ACT IV

Hell

Lucifer, in chains.

LUCIFER: Since love has come into the world my power is dead. Abel, who was delivered by Cain, had procreated with his sister.
    And I wish to deliver them all! Waters, seas, springs, rivers, you who are able to extinguish the flame of life: rise! exterminate!

ACT V

Heaven

God and Uriel.

URIEL: Woe unto us! Our joy is ended.
GOD: What has happened?
URIEL: Lucifer has breathed upon the waters; they rise and deliver the mortals!
GOD: I know! But I have saved two of the least enlightened, who will never know the key to the mystery. Their vessel has come ashore on Mount Ararat and they have made burnt offerings.
URIEL: But Lucifer has given them a plant called the vine, whose juice besots. A drop of wine, and they see things as they are.

GOD: Lunatics! They do not know that I have endowed their plant with strange properties: madness, sleep, and forgetfulness. With this plant they will no longer know what their eyes have seen.

URIEL: Woe unto us! What are they doing down there, fools who inhabit the earth?

GOD: They are building a tower and they wish to storm the heavens. Ha! Lucifer has taught them to question. Be it so! I shall confound their tongues so that their questions remain unanswered and my brother Lucifer be struck dumb!

ACT VI

Heaven

God and Uriel.

URIEL: Woe unto us! Lucifer has sent them his only son who teaches the truth to mankind . . .

GOD: What does he say?

URIEL: Born of a virgin, this son claims to have come to liberate mankind, and by his own death, he claims he will abolish the fear of death.

GOD: What does mankind say?

URIEL: Some say that the Son is God, others that he is the devil.

GOD: What do they mean by the devil?

URIEL: Lucifer!

GOD: (*Enraged.*) I regret having made man on the earth; he has become stronger than I, and I no longer know how to rule this pack of fools and madmen. Amaimon, Egyn, Paymon, Oriens, take this burden from me: tip the globe over pell-mell into the abyss! Malediction on the heads of the rebels! On the brow of the cursed planet fix the gallows, mark of crime, and of punishment and of suffering.

(*Enter Egyn and Amaimon.*)

EGYN: Lord! Your cruel will and bidding have produced their effect! The Earth careens in its orbit; the mountains crumble, the waters cover the earth; the axis turns to the north, to the cold and darkness; plague and famine ravage the nations; love has changed to mortal hate, filial devotion to parricide. Mankind believes itself in hell, and you, Lord, are dethroned!

GOD: Help! I repent having repented!

AMAIMON: Too late! There is no stopping any of it once you have unchained the forces . . .

GOD: I repent! I have implanted sparks of my soul in impure beings, whose fornication debases me as the wife, by defiling her body, defiles her husband.

EGYN: (*To Amaimon.*) The old man is delirious!

GOD: My energy gives out when they depart from me; their iniquity takes hold of me; and I am afflicted by the madness of my progeny. What have I done, Eternal One? Have pity on me! . . . Because he has loved curses, may curses fall upon him; and because he has delighted not in blessings, may blessings be ever distant from him!

EGYN: What madness!

GOD: (*Prostrate.*) Lord, Eternal One, there is none amongst the gods like unto thee; and thy works are incomparable. For thou art great, and thou dost wondrous things; and thou alone art God, thou alone!

AMAIMON: Madness!

EGYN: So goes the world: when the gods are amused, the mortals are abused!

. . .

END

Pierrot
Assassin of His Wife

Paul Margueritte

CHARACTERS:

Pierrot
An Undertaker's Man

[The passages in brackets appeared in the edition of 1910.]

Written and published 1882
First performances: Théâtre de Valvins, Seine-et-Marne, 1882
                  Théâtre Libre, Paris, March 23, 1888
                  with Margueritte as Pierrot and
                  Antoine as the Undertaker's Man
Translated by Daniel Gerould

Head and hands, plaster white, protrude from a white blouse, low-necked and pleated, with huge buttons. The head has sharply etched features, eyes in black, lips in red: thus the look in the right eye—the other is closed—and the laugh puckering a single corner of the mouth acquire animation. Forehead enlarged by a white head-band which is capped by a second band—the traditional one—in black velvet. The hands, also plaster white, and the wrists, beneath the ample and flowing sleeves, have narrow cuffs. Wide trousers which disclose his instep and his shoes with silver buckles.

N.B. Pierrot seems to speak?—Pure literary fiction!—Pierrot is mute, and this drama, from start to finish, mimed.

CURTAIN

The room with its dark paneling of old oak is dim and gloomy; against the wall, here a clothes chest, there a set of open shelves; a chair to the right, a table to the left, bottles on the floor, their necks broken. And drawing and holding the eye, back there, to the rear, a portrait of Colombine and a bed. Bed and portrait stand out from the shadows with astonishing relief and, although dead things, give the impression of life. Colombine in her frame of gold, all warm flesh, breasts bare, laughs with gusto, quite alive: there are portraits like this in Hoffmann. The bed too causes anxiety by the folds of its curtains which are drawn like those in cataflaques and reddish in hue. Music soft and strange, that could be said to be the harmonious expression of such a dwelling: Colombine's laughter and the breathing of her crimson bed are imaginatively portrayed in it. Some time passes. A door is flung open: through it there appears the sweaty and blood-tinged mug of an undertaker's man. He drags Pierrot along. Tall, supple, white of a classic whiteness—such is Pierrot. Pierrot staggers and plunges into the void, each step is a genuflexion: his legs are made of rubber; his arms, like wings, hang abandoned in the air. His momentary weakness is ambiguous: is it drunkenness? or despondency? In this fashion the two men come forward—the gross living human being and the spectral figure—with measured steps, black, white.

PIERROT: Whew! (*He sways, folds double, lifts a leg over a chair and falls back in it, in a swoon. The Undertaker's Man rubs Pierrot's hands briskly, and he revives.*) Oh! Over there! Look! Colombine! She's smiling, how graceful she looks! (*His extended arm points to the portrait.*) What eyes, what a pretty little nose! what a mouth . . . Dead. Alas! And we have just come back from out there where we consigned her to the earth. You remember: the pickaxe, the shovel, the gaping hole, the dirt thrown in after (*facing Pierrot and at the same time as Pierrot, the Undertaker's Man mimes the funeral scene*), and the prayers and the sobs. Dead! Dead! Oh! I shall never be consoled! (*He weeps.*) Never! (*And sinks back into a state of unconsciousness and displays the heart-rending silhouette of his body, bent at a right angle over the chair, arms and legs rigid. Come! Come! You must be reasonable! objects the Undertaker's Man who, in a compassionate gesture, dries Pierrot's eyes. The stench of the handkerchief acting as smelling salts, Pierrot rouses himself indignantly, sneezes, throws the rag in the man's face: for all that, he does not squeeze the man's hands any less tightly.*) There! It's true, I must resign myself and be a man . . . Ah! . . . There! Shouldn't we take heart and be brave. A small glass of cognac, eh? (*The Undertaker's Man nods assent; Pierrot goes to the sideboard and fills two small glasses. To your health! says the Undertaker's Man.*) Oh, no! To her, to the health of the deceased! (*And both of them raise their glasses towards the portrait.*) Well! That's funny, not bad, this cognac, quite good even! (*And Pierrot who has kept the decanter in his hand, smacking his tongue against his lips, pours himself small glassfulls one after the other.*) Good! Very good, delicious, damned if it isn't! (*The Undertaker's Man lured on and vainly extending his glass, is rash enough to pull Pierrot by the sleeve, causing him to burst out.*) Hey! What does that mean? You dare ask for another glass of my cognac (by the way, perfectly delicious!) . . . drunkard! to insult the dead and in this room, you wretch! Get out . . . Get out this instant! (*The Undertaker's Man failing to respond quickly enough to Pierrot's arguments is showered with blows and ignominiously driven out by means of kicks in the ass. Alone, Pierrot bursts into a long laugh, convulsively. Calmer, he opens his mouth, is on the verge of making a full confession, but mistrustful, he stops short. However, slowly ravaged by the idea that obsesses him, there pass across his face within a few seconds impressions of fear, anger, sadness, and astonishment. The secret, for a second time, comes to his lips: what frightful thing is Pierrot about to say? Nothing, because he stops short once again and craftily changes the subject.*) I'm sleepy. I feel weary. Suppose we go to sleep. Suppose we get undressed. First, my shoes . . . (*He sits down and takes his foot in his hand.*) Hey! (*He turns around abrupt and fearful.*) What was that? No! . . . Ah! Ah! . . . imbecile, there's nothing. (*He shrugs his shoulders and takes hold of his other foot.*) Ah! Now this time! (*He gets up, looks under the chair, under the table, under the bed, opens its curtains and draws back before this empty bed, full of terror.*) I remember! (*He stares at the portrait and points at it with a mysterious finger.*) I remember . . . Close the curtains! I dare not . . .

(*He backs up to the bed and with his arms held out behind him, not looking, he draws the draperies. His lips quiver and then an invincible force wrests from Pierrot the secret already filling his mouth. The music stops and listens.*)

This is the story:

Colombine, my darling, my wife, the Colombine of the portrait, was sleeping. She was sleeping, there, in the great bed: I killed her. Why? . . . Ah, of course! She pinched my gold; my best wine she drank; my back she gave a drubbing, and a thorough one at that; as for my forehead, she decorated it with horns. A cuckold, yes, that's what she made me, a cuckold, and with a vengeance, but what does that matter? I killed her; because I felt like it, I am the master here, any one have any objections? Kill her, yes . . . That strikes my fancy. But how am I going to do it? (*Because Pierrot, as somnambulant, re-enacts his crime, and in his hallucination, the past becomes the present.*) Of course there's always the rope, you pull it tight, snap, it's all over! Yes, but the tongue hanging out, the face turned horrible? No.—The knife? Or a sabre, a huge sabre? Slash! Through the heart . . . Yes, but the blood flows in torrents, it gushes out.—Whew! I'll be damned! . . . Poison? A tiny vial of nothing at all, swallow it and then . . . Yes! And then the cramps, the wracking pains, the agonies, ah, it's horrible (besides, it could be detected). Of course there is always the gun, bang! But that bang! would be heard. —Nothing, I come up with nothing. (*He paces about solemnly and meditates. Accidentally he stumbles.*) Ouch, that hurts! (*He rubs his foot.*) Ow! That hurts! It won't last, it's better now. (*He keeps rubbing and tickling his foot.*) Ah! Ah! That's funny! Ah! Ah! No! It makes you laugh. Ah! (*He suddenly lets go of his foot. He strikes his forehead.*) I've got it! (*Slyly.*) I've got it! I'll tickle my wife to death, that's it! Tickle her ever so nicely, that's it! What a clever idea. Ah! Yes, but don't get carried away, easy; let's go at this step by step . . . (*Stealthily, he approaches the crimson bed and listens.*) She's sleeping, good! (*He half-opens the curtains and peeps in.*) She's sleeping soundly—careful! (*He pulls the curtains along their rod, but instead of sliding, the rings grate: Pierrot jumps.*) Hum! It's a tricky business: easy! Eas . . . (*The rings grate horribly.*) Confound it! (*And abruptly, risking all, he opens the curtains wide all at once, and leaning over—at the head of the bed, actually empty, but where she is, where she is for him—he peers in.*) Nothing! She has not stirred. She is still sleeping. There, love, here is a kiss! Hee! Hee! How pretty she is, asleep: a tiny face, darling little eyes, a nose no bigger than that, breasts that arch, a haunch firmly etched . . . (*Here Pierrot, having yielded for a moment to retrospective concupiscence, snaps out of it.*) Let's get going! First some rope (*he ties Colombine up with an imaginary rope*) so that you won't be able to stir, with either arms or legs—next a gag (*he rolls up an imaginary handkerchief and puts it over the mouth of the woman who isn't there*) and now (*he lifts up the sheet and slides his hands under the covers which begin to shake*) to work! Pretty smile, pretty little smile, please; good morning, Colombine . . . (*He flings himself full length on the bed and, transforming himself, imparts to his body the rigidity of a trussed-up body, he frantically waves his tickled feet, he frees his mouth from the bandage, he becomes Colombine, he is Colombine. She wakes up.*) It's you, Pierrot, ah! ah! you're tickling me, oh! oh! oh! stop, ah! stop! ah! ah! ah! I'm going to break the rope, oh! oh! oh! You're hurting me! . . . ah! ah! you're hurting me! . . . (*Pierrot flings himself back to the foot of the bed and resumes his tickling, not saying a word, not laughing, with a gallow's look. Suddenly, he stops.*) I heard . . . (*He comes forward, holds one hand to his ear, the other to his heart.*) I hear . . . what is it then? My heart is pounding. Fast. Faster! And faster! (*And his hand indicates his accelerating heart beat, and his eye, in its socket, haggard and terrified, gleams.*) The noise is subsiding. My heart is pounding. Slower! And slower! With a steady beat. There. Nothing any more. (*His hands fall back down.*) I had a good scare. Now, back to tickling: Colombine, you're going to pay for that. (*And he tickles recklessly, he tickles savagely, he tickles anew, he tickles without respite, then he flings himself onto the bed and becomes Colombine once more. She [he] writhes in frightful gaiety. One of her [his] arms gets free and frees the other arm, and these two arms, in a state of dementia, curse Pierrot. She [he] bursts into a laugh, genuine, strident, mortal; and raises herself [himself] part way; and tries to fling herself [himself] out of the bed; and her [his] feet keep on dancing, tickled, tortured, epileptic. These are the death-pangs. She [he] rises up once or twice—the supreme spasm—opens her [his] mouth for a final curse, and lets fall backwards, across the bed, her [his] head and arms dangling down. Pierrot becomes Pierrot again. At the foot of the bed, he scratches some more, worn out, gasping for breath, but victorious. He is amazed.*) What! Nothing more! She's stopped moving! Is she dead! Yes, but really and truly! Let's look a bit more closely: heart? Quite still. Pulse? Not a trace. Eyes? Up-turned. Tongue? Hanging out. Dead! It's all over. Let's put things in order. First the head, on the pillow: let's fix the expression. (*Under Pierrot's sacrilegious fingers, the dead woman's face gradually grows peaceful and smiling.*) Off wth the ropes. Now, there's the bed to tuck in, the wrinkles to smooth out, it's all done, nothing else, no tell-tale signs. Colombine, as she did not long ago, sleeps, ever so pretty. There! Over, over, it's all over. (*He closes the curtains, and does an about-face. Winking with one eye, given over to pure joy, a pale smile on his lunar visage, he rubs his hands, at length.*) Dead! Quite dead, and not a thing, not a single thing will be discovered! The gendarme, with his huge sabre and his moustaches, if he comes and knocks at my door, bang! bang! I go to open it. He grabs me by the collar. Me? Oh, gendarme, look: there she is, dead in her bed, ever so prettily: I wash my hands of the whole affair, do you understand. And prison, handcuffs, bolted cell doors, not for me, not that either: dead in her bed, no concern of mine. And the guillotine. Swoosh! The whirring blade, my head spinning off . . . ah! But no, that's not for me! Ah! Ah! Ah! (*And Pierrot laughs silently, for a long while. Torpor invades his body, immobilizing him and congealing his limbs: his eyes close, and his head droops while his lips of plaster retain their satisfied, ironic smile. Music. He starts abruptly, looks around him, stretches.)*

Phew! I feel weary, tired out, I've surely earned the right to sleep, at present. *(He yawns.)* Rock-a-bye-baby! On the tree top! *(Music for a lullaby.)* Let's get undressed. *(He sits down.)* My shoes . . . *(But when, exactly as before, he goes to take his shoes off, he sees with stupefaction, then fright, his foot shaken by an involuntary dance, by a convulsive trembling like that of an alcoholic. This trembling spreads, seizes the other foot and the other leg. Pierrot stands up and shakes. No doubt about it! Like a contagious and vengeful disease, the tickling of Colombine has him in its grip. Pierrot runs about the room in all directions on tiptoe. His arms, wide as wings, beat the air, mad and tragic.)* Stop, oh, for pity's sake, stop, my feet . . . *(The trembling ceases. Pierrot sinks back down on the soles of his feet and looking grim, makes a sudden decision.)* What to do? Ah! Drink! That's the cure, that's what I need. *(And he mimes expressively.)* Yes, one glass, two glasses, down the hatch, let's drink up, another and another! Until we're rolling on the floor, no longer seeing or hearing anything, drunk, dead . . . Oh, no! Ugh! That's not what I want. *(But the music breaks loose; and once again the horrible trembling shakes Pierrot's feet; panic-stricken, he cannot keep his teeth from chattering.)* Oh, no! Not that again! Not again! *(He flings himself on his knees in front of the portrait, which continues to smile and look implacable.)* Colombine, mercy, pardon, pity! I prefer drinking, I am going to drink! *(He goes over to the table and places the bottles on it. Then, with a grandeur found in antique gesture, he invokes the sovereign good of Drunkenness.)* Flagons, full of exquisite wine, I shall drink you: lull me to sleep, give me drunkenness, dreams, annihilation, be merciful, flagons, which I implore, which I kiss . . . *(He drinks. Music, lazy and hushed. He drinks slowly and deeply.)* One! *(Throws the emptied bottle over his shoulder.)* Hideous wine! *(Even drunkenness fails Pierrot, the wine sickens him.)* Let's drink! *(He takes a second bottle, it is champagne.)* Yes, this one will be better. *(In the meantime, the wine he has drunk has had its effect, Pierrot's eye grows animated, his face brightens; the music too becomes gay. He has cut the wire and is about to pop the cork, he stops just in time.)* Halt! Patience! Gulp it down all at once? Oh! no, let's savor it. *(He contemplates the bottle with tenderness and cries out.)* I shall drink it five times, I shall take possession of it five times. First, with the eyes *(he examines it and admires it)*, what pretty color!—With the hands: I want to caress it, like a woman's hand *(he caresses it)*, how soft it is!—The ear. Let's listen. *(He sits down, holds the bottle to his ear, then places it between his legs, astonished and delighted.)* Yes, it talks, it sings. *(The music meanders.)* These are songs for the violin, songs for the flute, songs for the piano!—Now it's the nose's turn. *(He sniffs the bottle, remaining seated—the bouquet entices him, vertiginously—the bottle dances in his hand and gives him a spasm which agitates his arm, his head, and his legs, lasciviously, and which ends in a swoon.)*—The tongue finally, let us drink! *(And Pierrot pops the cork, laps the overflowing froth, and drinks volup-*

tuously.) Ah! How good that is! It goes right down into your veins, it circulates, it flies up to your brain, it warms you up, it makes you gay! To your health, Colombine! (*He drinks an ironic toast to the portrait, then eyes the conjugal bed with a wanton look.*) Ah! ah! there, Colombine, I kiss you, I take you in my arms, I hold you . . . (*Pierrot grows dejected. The effervescent drunkenness caused by the champagne is already wearing off.*) I'm cold, it's getting dark and sad. (*Night comes on, the music grows solemn.*) Brrr! (*He goes and breaks the neck of the last bottle on the edge of the table.*) Let's drink, it's the end. (*He drinks, standing upright, and falls back down in a heap, on the chair. Night has fallen. Nothing can be seen but a vague, white Pierrot. He gets up slowly [a candle in his hand] and crosses the room, a wavering shape, with irresolute gestures. He finally goes to undress, to lie down, to get into his bed, when terror glues him to the spot. What's happened is that, suffering from hallucinations caused by involuntary and all-powerful Remorse, Pierrot thinks he sees—and actually does see—the BED, lost in the shadows, grow animated and illuminated like an enormous lantern and come to life; and the somber curtains turn crimson and gradually burst into flames and blaze. Pierrot passes his hand over his forehead. [He changes the position of the candle.] The vision is gone. The bed is plunged in darkness, once again. But now, a new and greater source of anguish, the PORTRAIT comes to life. First the frame glows, phosphorescent, afterwards Colombine lights up: her laughter rings out, red and white. She lives, truly she lives and she laughs at Pierrot . . . she laughed that way when Pierrot killed her . . . Then, before the portrait, he backs away mechanically, with rigid steps. He stops. He is angry at himself for his own cowardice. He tells himself to be brave. He will be brave. He moves forward, arms extended. He glides, spectral, already dead, towards the dead woman. HE TOUCHES HER! The music, at the shattering call of a gong, goes mad. [Pierrot's teeth chatter, his hand catches unawares on the bed, which the candle sets on fire.] The bed too lights up and once more turns crimson. Pierrot, in the red light, twists his body, seized with madness. Three times he spins completely around: his arms rove, his fingers claw the void. What has happened is that the old convulsive trembling, the horrible tickling now frantically shake his body, and in the final, funereal sob stuck in his throat can be heard the old laughter, exactly the laugh of Colombine's death throes . . . Then suddenly, at the feet of his painted victim who never stops laughing, at a single stroke, falling backwards and with arms crosswise, Pierrot's corpse comes crashing down.*)

END

The Intruder

Maurice Maeterlinck

CHARACTERS:

The Grandfather, blind.
The Father
The Three Daughters
The Uncle
The Sister of Mercy
The Maid

The scene is set in modern times.

Written and published 1890
First performance: Théâtre de l'Art, Paris, May 21, 1891
                    with Lugné-Poe as the Father
Revised version of an anonymous translation first published in 1892

A somber room in an old chateau. A door on the right, a door on the left, and a small concealed door in a corner. At the back, stained-glass windows, in which green is the dominant color, and a glass door opening onto a terrace. A large Dutch clock in one corner. A lighted lamp.

THE THREE DAUGHTERS: Come here, grandfather. Sit down under the lamp.

THE GRANDFATHER: It does not seem to me to be very light here.

THE FATHER: Shall we go out on the terrace, or stay in this room?

THE UNCLE: Would it not be better to stay here? It has rained the whole week, and the nights are damp and cold.

THE ELDEST DAUGHTER: But the stars are shining.

THE UNCLE: Oh, the stars—that's nothing.

THE GRANDFATHER: We had better stay here. One never knows what may happen.

THE FATHER: There is no longer any cause for anxiety. The danger is past, and she is saved . . .

THE GRANDFATHER: I believe she is not doing so well . . .

THE FATHER: Why do you say that?

THE GRANDFATHER: I have heard her voice.

THE FATHER: But since the doctors assure us that we need not worry . . .

THE UNCLE: You know quite well that your father-in-law likes to alarm us needlessly.

THE GRANDFATHER: I don't see things as you do.

THE UNCLE: Then you ought to rely on those who can see. She looked very well this afternoon. She is sleeping quietly now; and we are not going to spoil the first pleasant evening that chance has put in our way. . . . It seems to me we have a perfect right to peace, and even to laugh a little this evening, without being afraid.

THE FATHER: That's true; this is the first time I have felt at home with my family since this terrible childbirth.

THE UNCLE: Once illness has come into a house, it is as though a stranger had forced himself into the family circle.

THE FATHER: And then you understand, too, that you can count on no one outside the family.

THE UNCLE: You are quite right.

THE GRANDFATHER: Why couldn't I see my poor daughter today?

THE UNCLE: You know quite well—the doctor forbade it.

THE GRANDFATHER: I do not know what to think . . .

THE UNCLE: It is useless to worry.

THE GRANDFATHER: (*Pointing to the door on the left.*) She cannot hear us?

THE FATHER: We will not talk too loud; besides, the door is very thick, and the Sister of Mercy is with her, and she is sure to warn us if we are making too much noise.

GRANDFATHER: (*Pointing to the door on the right.*) He cannot hear us?

THE FATHER: No, no.

THE GRANDFATHER: He is asleep?

THE FATHER: I suppose so.

THE GRANDFATHER: Someone had better go and see.

THE UNCLE: The little one would cause *me* more anxiety than your wife. It is now several weeks since he was born, and he has scarcely stirred. He has not cried once all the time. He is like a wax doll.

THE GRANDFATHER: I think he will be deaf, and dumb too, perhaps . . . That's the usual result of a marriage between cousins . . . (*A reproachful silence.*)

THE FATHER: I could almost wish him ill for the suffering he has caused his mother.

THE UNCLE: Do be reasonable; it is not the poor little thing's fault. He is all alone in the room?

THE FATHER: Yes; the doctor does not want him to stay in his mother's room any longer.

THE UNCLE: But the nurse is with him?

THE FATHER: No; she has gone to rest a little; she has well deserved it these last few days. Ursula, just go and see if he is asleep.

THE ELDEST DAUGHER: Yes, father. (*The Three Sisters get up, and go into the room on the right, hand in hand.*)

THE FATHER: When will our sister come?

THE UNCLE: I think she will come about nine.

THE FATHER: It is past nine. I hope she will come this evening; my wife is so anxious to see her.

THE UNCLE: She is sure to come. This will be the first time she has been here?

THE FATHER: She has never been in the house.

THE UNCLE: It is very difficult for her to leave her convent.

THE FATHER: Will she be alone?

THE UNCLE: I expect one of the nuns will come with her. They are not allowed to go out alone.

THE FATHER: But she is the Superior.

THE UNCLE: The rule is the same for all.

THE GRANDFATHER: Do you not feel anxious?

THE UNCLE: Why should we feel anxious? What's the good of harping on that? There is nothing more to fear.

THE GRANDFATHER: Your sister is older than you?

THE UNCLE: She is the eldest.

THE GRANDFATHER: I do not know what is the matter with me; I feel uneasy. I wish your sister were here.

THE UNCLE: She will come; she promised to.

THE GRANDFATHER: Ah, if this evening were only over! (*The three daughters come in again.*)

THE FATHER: He is asleep?

THE ELDEST DAUGHTER: Yes, father; he is sleeping soundly.

THE UNCLE: What shall we do while we are waiting?

THE GRANDFATHER: Waiting for what?

THE UNCLE: Waiting for our sister.

THE FATHER: You see nothing coming, Ursula?

THE ELDEST DAUGHTER: (*At the window.*) Nothing, father.

THE FATHER: Not in the avenue? Can you see the avenue?

THE DAUGHTER: Yes, father; the moon is out, and I can see the avenue as far as the cypress groves.

THE GRANDFATHER: And you see no one?

THE DAUGHTER: No one, grandfather.

THE UNCLE: What sort of a night is it?

THE DAUGHTER: Very fine. Do you hear the nightingales?

THE UNCLE: Yes, yes.

THE DAUGHTER: A little wind is rising in the avenue.

THE GRANDFATHER: A little wind in the avenue?

THE DAUGHTER: Yes; the trees are trembling a little.

THE UNCLE: I am surprised that my sister is not here yet.

THE GRANDFATHER: I cannot hear the nightingales any more.

THE DAUGHTER: I think someone has come into the garden, grandfather.

THE GRANDFATHER: Who is it?

THE DAUGHTER: I do not know; I can see no one.

THE UNCLE: Because there is no one there.

THE DAUGHTER: There must be someone in the garden; the nightingales have suddenly stopped singing.

THE GRANDFATHER: But I do not hear anyone coming.

THE DAUGHTER: Someone must be passing by the pond, because the swans are frightened.

ANOTHER DAUGHTER: All the fishes in the pond are diving suddenly.

THE FATHER: You see no one?

THE DAUGHTER: No one, father.

THE FATHER: But the pond lies in the moonlight . . .

THE DAUGHTER: Yes; I can see that the swans are frightened.

THE UNCLE: I am sure it is my sister who is frightening them. She must have come in by the little gate.

THE FATHER: I cannot understand why the dogs do not bark.

THE DAUGHTER: I can see the watchdog right at the back of his kennel. The swans are crossing to the other bank! . . .

THE UNCLE: They are afraid of my sister. I will go and see. (*He calls.*) Sister! Sister! Is that you? . . . There is no one there.

THE DAUGHTER: I am sure that someone has come into the garden. You will see.

THE UNCLE: But she would answer me!

THE GRANDFATHER: Are not the nightingales beginning to sing again, Ursula?

THE DAUGHTER: I cannot hear one anywhere.

THE GRANDFATHER: But there is no noise.

THE FATHER: There is a silence of the grave.

THE GRANDFATHER: It must be a stranger who is frightening them, for if it were one of the family, they would not be silent.

THE UNCLE: How much longer are you going to discuss these nightingales?

THE GRANDFATHER: Are all the windows open, Ursula?

THE DAUGHTER: The glass door is open, grandfather.

THE GRANDFATHER: It seems to me that the cold is coming into the room.

THE DAUGHTER: There is a little wind in the garden, grandfather, and the rose petals are falling.

THE FATHER: Well, then, shut the door. It is late.

THE DAUGHTER: Yes, father.—I cannot shut the door.

THE TWO OTHER DAUGHTERS: We cannot shut the door.

THE GRANDFATHER: Why, what is the matter with the door, my children?

THE UNCLE: You need not say that in such an extraordinary voice. I will go and help them.

THE ELDEST DAUGHTER: We cannot manage to shut it tight.

THE UNCLE: It is because of the damp. Let us all push together. There must be something in the way.

THE FATHER: The carpenter will fix it tomorrow.

THE GRANDFATHER: Is the carpenter coming tomorrow?

THE DAUGHTER: Yes, grandfather; he is coming to do some work in the cellar.

THE GRANDFATHER: He will make noise in the house! . . .

THE DAUGHTER: I will tell him to work quietly.

(*Suddenly the sound of a scythe being sharpened is heard outside.*)

THE GRANDFATHER: (*With a shudder.*) Oh!

THE UNCLE: What is that?

THE DAUGHTER: I don't exactly know; I think it is the gardener. I cannot see very well; he is in the shadow of the house.

THE FATHER: It is the gardener going to mow.

THE UNCLE: He mows at night?

THE FATHER: Is not tomorrow Sunday?—Yes.—I noticed that the grass was very high around the house.

THE GRANDFATHER: It seems to me that his scythe makes a great deal of noise . . .

THE DAUGHTER: He is mowing near the house.

THE GRANDFATHER: Can you see him, Ursula?

THE DAUGHTER: No, grandfather. He is in the dark.

THE GRANDFATHER: I am afraid he will wake my daughter.

THE UNCLE: We can scarcely hear him.

THE GRANDFATHER: It sounds to me as if he were mowing inside the house.

THE UNCLE: She will not hear it; there is no danger.

THE FATHER: It seems to me that the lamp is not burning well tonight.

THE UNCLE: It needs filling.

THE FATHER: I saw it filled this morning. It has burnt badly since the window was shut.

THE UNCLE: I think the chimney is dirty.

THE FATHER: It will burn better soon.

THE DAUGHTER: Grandfather has fallen asleep. He has not slept for three nights.

THE FATHER: He has been so worried.

THE UNCLE: He always worries too much. At times he will not listen to reason.

THE FATHER: It is quite excusable at his age.

THE UNCLE: God knows what we shall be like at his age.

THE FATHER: He is nearly eighty.

THE UNCLE: Then he has a right to be strange.

THE FATHER: He is like all blind people.

THE UNCLE: They think too much.

THE FATHER: They have too much time to spare.

THE UNCLE: They have nothing else to do.

THE FATHER: And, besides, they have no distractions.

THE UNCLE: It must be terrible.

THE FATHER: Apparently they get used to it.

THE UNCLE: I cannot imagine it.

THE FATHER: They are certainly to be pitied.

THE UNCLE: Not to know where one is, not to know where one has come from, not to know where one is going, not to be able to tell midday from midnight, or summer from winter—and always the darkness, the darkness! I would rather not live. Is it absolutely incurable?

THE FATHER: Apparently so.

THE UNCLE: But he is not absolutely blind?

THE FATHER: He can perceive a strong light.

THE UNCLE: Let us take care of our poor eyes.

THE FATHER: He often has strange ideas.

THE UNCLE: At times he is not at all amusing.

THE FATHER: He says absolutely everything he thinks.

THE UNCLE: But he was not always like this?

THE FATHER: No; once he was as rational as we are; he never said anything extraordinary. I am afraid Ursula encourages him a little too much; she answers all his questions . . .

THE UNCLE: It would be better not to answer them. It's a mistaken kindness to him.

(Ten o'clock strikes.)

THE GRANDFATHER: (Waking up.) Am I facing the glass door?

THE DAUGHTER: You have had a nice sleep, grandfather?

THE GRANDFATHER: Am I facing the glass door?

THE DAUGHTER: Yes, grandfather.

THE GRANDFATHER: There is no one at the glass door?

THE DAUGHTER: No, grandfather; I see no one.

THE GRANDFATHER: I thought someone was waiting. No one has come?

THE DAUGHTER: No one, grandfather.

THE GRANDFATHER: (To the Uncle and Father.) And your sister has not come?

THE UNCLE: It is too late; she will not come now. It is not nice of her.

THE FATHER: I'm beginning to worry about her. (A noise, as of someone coming into the house.)

THE UNCLE: There she is! Did you hear?

THE FATHER: Yes; someone has come in through the basement.

THE UNCLE: It must be our sister. I recognized her step.

THE GRANDFATHER: I heard slow footsteps.

THE FATHER: She came in very quietly.

THE UNCLE: She knows there is someone sick here.

THE GRANDFATHER: I hear nothing now.

THE UNCLE: She will come up directly; they will tell her we are here.

THE FATHER: I am glad she has come.

THE UNCLE: I was sure she would come tonight.

THE GRANDFATHER: She is slow in coming up.

THE UNCLE: It must be she.

THE FATHER: We are not expecting any other visitors.

THE GRANDFATHER: I cannot hear any noise in the basement.

THE FATHER: I will call the servant. We shall see how things stand. (He pulls a *bell-rope.*)

THE GRANDFATHER: I can hear a noise on the stairs already.

THE FATHER: It is the maid coming up.

THE GRANDFATHER: It seems to me that she is not alone.

THE FATHER: She is coming up slowly . . .

THE GRANDFATHER: I hear your sister's step!

THE FATHER: I can only hear the maid.

THE GRANDFATHER: It is your sister! It is your sister! (*There is a knock at the little door.*)

THE UNCLE: She is knocking at the door of the back stairs.

THE FATHER: I will go and open it myself, because that little door makes too much noise; we use it only when we want to come up without being seen. (*He opens the little door partly; the Maid remains outside in the opening.*) Where are you?

THE MAID: Here, sir.

THE GRANDFATHER: Your sister is at the door?

THE UNCLE: I can only see the maid.

THE FATHER: It is only the maid. (*To the Maid.*) Who was that who came into the house?

THE MAID: Came into the house?

THE FATHER: Yes; someone came in just now?

THE MAID: No one came in, sir.

THE GRANDFATHER: Who is it sighing like that?

THE UNCLE: It is the maid; she is out of breath.

THE GRANDFATHER: Is she crying?

THE UNCLE: No; why should she be crying?

THE FATHER: (*To the Maid.*) No one came in just now?

THE MAID: No, sir.

THE FATHER: But we heard someone open the door!

THE MAID: It was I shutting the door.

THE FATHER: It was open?

THE MAID: Yes, sir.

THE FATHER: Why was it open at this time of night?

THE MAID: I do not know, sir. I had shut it myself.

THE FATHER: Then who was it that opened it?

THE MAID: I do not know, sir. Someone must have gone out after me, sir . . .

THE FATHER: You must be careful.—Don't push the door like that; you know what a noise it makes!

THE MAID: But, sir, I am not touching the door.

THE FATHER: But you are. You are pushing as if you were trying to get into the room!

THE MAID: But sir, I am three steps away from the door!

THE FATHER: Don't talk so loud.

THE GRANDFATHER: Are they putting out the light?

THE ELDEST DAUGHTER: No, grandfather.

THE GRANDFATHER: It seems to me that it has suddenly grown dark.

THE FATHER: (*To the Maid.*) You can go down again now; but do not make so much noise on the stairs.

THE MAID: I did not make any noise.

THE FATHER: I tell you that you did make noise. Go down quietly; you might wake your mistress. And if anyone comes, say that we are not at home.

THE UNCLE: Yes, say that we are not at home.

THE GRANDFATHER: (*Shuddering.*) You must not say that!

THE FATHER: . . . Unless it's my sister or the doctor.

THE UNCLE: When will the doctor come?

THE FATHER: He will not be able to come before midnight. (*He shuts the door. A clock is heard striking eleven.*)

THE GRANDFATHER: She has come in?

THE FATHER: Who?

THE GRANDFATHER: The maid.

THE FATHER: No, she has gone downstairs.

THE GRANDFATHER: I thought that she was sitting at the table.

THE UNCLE: The maid.

THE GRANDFATHER: Yes.

THE UNCLE: That's all we would need!

THE GRANDFATHER: No one has come into the room?

THE FATHER: No; no one has come in.

THE GRANDFATHER: And your sister is not here?

THE UNCLE: Our sister has not come.

THH GRANDFATHER: You want to deceive me!

THE UNCLE: Deceive you?

THE GRANDFATHER: Ursula, for the love of God, tell me the truth!

THE ELDEST DAUGHTER: Grandfather! Grandfather! What is the matter with you?

THE GRANDFATHER: Something has happened. I am sure my daughter is worse! . . .

THE UNCLE: Are you dreaming?

THE GRANDFATHER: You do not want to tell me! . . . I can see quite well that something has happened . . .

THE UNCLE: In that case you can see better than we can.

THE GRANDFATHER: Ursula, tell me the truth!

THE DAUGHTER: But we have told you the truth, grandfather!

THE GRANDFATHER: You are not speaking in your ordinary voice.

THE FATHER: That is because you've been frightening her.

THE GRANDFATHER: Your voice has changed, too.

THE FATHER: You are going mad! (*He and the Uncle make signs to each other to signify the Grandfather has lost his reason.)*

THE GRANDFATHER: I can hear quite well that you are afraid.

THE FATHER: But what should we be afraid of?

THE GRANDFATHER: Why do you want to deceive me?

THE UNCLE: Who is thinking of deceiving you?

THE GRANDFATHER: Why have you put out the light?

THE UNCLE: But the light has not been put out; there is as much light as there was before.

THE DAUGHTER: It seems to me that the lamp has gone down.

THE FATHER: I see as well now as ever.

THE GRANDFATHER: I have millstones on my eyes! Tell me, girls, what is going on here! Tell me, for the love of God, you who can see! I am here, all alone, in darkness without end! I do not know who is sitting down beside me! I do not know what is happening two steps from me! . . . Why were you talking in a low voice just now?

THE FATHER: No one was talking in a low voice.

THE GRANDFATHER: You did talk in a low voice at the door.

THE FATHER: You heard everything I said.

THE GRANDFATHER: You brought someone into the room!

THE FATHER: But I tell you no one has come in!

THE GRANDFATHER: Is it your sister or a priest?—You should not try to deceive me.—Ursula, who was it that came in?

THE DAUGHTER: No one, grandfather.

THE GRANDFATHER: You must not try to deceive me; I know what I know!—How many of us are there here?

THE DAUGHTER: There are six of us around the table, grandfather.

THE GRANDFATHER: You are all around the table?

THE DAUGHTER: Yes, grandfather.

THE GRANDFATHER: Are you there, Paul?

THE FATHER: Yes.

THE GRANDFATHER: Are you there, Oliver?

THE UNCLE: Yes, of course I am here, in my usual place. You are joking, aren't you?

THE GRANDFATHER: Are you there, Geneviève?

ONE OF THE DAUGHTERS: Yes, grandfather.

THE GRANDFATHER: Are you there, Gertrude?

ANOTHER DAUGHTER: Yes, grandfather.

THE GRANDFATHER: Are you here, Ursula?

THE ELDEST DAUGHTER: Yes, grandfather, next to you.

THE GRANDFATHER: And who is that sitting there?

THE DAUGHTER: Where do you mean, grandfather?—There is no one.

THE GRANDFATHER: There, there, in the midst of us?

THE DAUGHTER: But there is no one, grandfather!

THE FATHER: We tell you there is no one!

THE GRANDFATHER: But you cannot see—any of you!

THE UNCLE: Come now! You are joking.

THE GRANDFATHER: I do not feel like joking, I can assure you.

THE UNCLE: Then believe those who can see.

THE GRANDFATHER: (*Undecidedly.*) I thought there was someone . . . I believe
  I shall not live much longer . . .

THE UNCLE: Why should we deceive you? What good would that do?

THE FATHER: It would be our duty to tell you the truth . . .

THE UNCLE: What good would it do to deceive each other?

THE FATHER: You'd find out the truth in no time.

THE GRANDFATHER: (*Trying to get up.*) I should like to pierce this darkness! . . .

THE FATHER: Where do you want to go?

THE GRANDFATHER: Over there . . .

THE FATHER: Don't be so anxious.

THE UNCLE: You are strange tonight.

THE GRANDFATHER: It is all of you who seem strange to me!

THE FATHER: What are you trying to find? . . .

THE GRANDFATHER: I do not know what is the matter with me!

THE ELDEST DAUGHTER: Grandfather! Grandfather! What do you want, grandfather?

THE GRANDFATHER: Give me your little hands, girls.

THE THREE DAUGHTERS: Yes, grandfather.

THE GRANDFATHER: Why are all three of you trembling, girls?

THE ELDEST DAUGHTER: We are scarcely trembling, grandfather.

THE GRANDFATHER: I believe all three of you are quite pale.

THE ELDEST DAUGHTER: It is late, grandfather, and we are tired.

THE FATHER: You must go to bed, and grandfather himself would do well to
  get a little rest.

THE GRANDFATHER: I could not sleep tonight!

THE UNCLE: We will wait for the doctor.

THE GRANDFATHER: Prepare me for the truth!

THE UNCLE: But there is no truth!

THE GRANDFATHER: Then I do not know what is the matter!

THE UNCLE: I tell you there is nothing the matter!

THE GRANDFATHER: I wish I could see my poor daughter!

THE FATHER: But you know quite well it is impossible; she must not be awakened needlessly.

THE UNCLE: You will see her tomorrow.

THE GRANDFATHER: There is no sound coming from her room.

THE UNCLE: I should be uneasy if I heard any sound.

THE GRANDFATHER: I have not seen my daughter for a very long time! . . . I
  held her hands yesterday evening, but I could not see her! . . . I do not know

what has happened to her . . . I do not know what she looks like . . . I do not know what her face is like anymore . . . She must have changed these past weeks! . . . I felt her small cheekbones with my hands . . . There is nothing but the darkness between her and me, and all of you! . . . I cannot go on living like this . . . This is not living! . . . You sit there, all of you, with eyes wide open looking into my dead eyes, and not one of you feels any pity! . . . I do not know what is the matter with me . . . No one ever says what should be said . . . And everything is terrifying when you think about it . . . But why don't you say something?

THE UNCLE: What should we say, since you will not believe us?

THE GRANDFATHER: You are afraid of betraying yourselves!

THE FATHER: Come now, be reasonable!

THE GRANDFATHER: You have been hiding something from me for a long time! . . . Something has happened in the house . . . But I am beginning to understand now . . . You have been deceiving me for too long!—You think that I shall never find out anything?—There are moments when I am less blind than you, you know! . . . Do you think I have not heard you whispering, for days and days, as if you were in the house of someone who had hanged himself?—I dare not say what I know tonight . . . But I shall know the truth! . . . I shall wait for you to tell me the truth; but I have known it for a long time, in spite of you!—And now, I feel that you are all paler than the dead!

THE THREE DAUGHTERS: Grandfather! Grandfather! What is the matter, grandfather?

THE GRANDFATHER: It is not you that I am speaking of, girls. No; it is not you that I am speaking of . . . I know quite well you would tell me the truth, if they were not here! . . . And besides, I feel sure that they are deceiving you as well . . . You will see, children, you will see! . . . Do I not hear all three of you sobbing?

THE FATHER: Is my wife really in danger?

THE GRANDFATHER: You mustn't try to deceive me any longer; it is too late now, and I know the truth better than you! . . .

THE UNCLE: But *we* are not blind; *we* are not!

THE FATHER: Would you like to go into your daughter's room? This misunderstanding must come to an end.—Would you like to?

THE GRANDFATHER: (*Suddenly hesitant.*) No, no, not now . . . not yet . . .

THE UNCLE: You see, you are not reasonable.

THE GRANDFATHER: One never knows all that a man has been unable to express during his life! . . . Who is making that noise?

THE ELDEST DAUGHTER: It is the lamp flickering, grandfather.

THE GRANDFATHER: It seems to me to be very unsteady . . . very unsteady . . .

THE DAUGHTER: It is the cold wind troubling it . . .

THE UNCLE: There is no cold wind, the windows are shut.

THE DAUGHTER: I think it is going out.

THE FATHER: There is no more oil.

THE DAUGHTER: It has gone completely out.

THE FATHER: We cannot stay like this in the dark.

THE UNCLE: Why not?—I am quite used to it.

THE FATHER: There is a light in my wife's room.

THE UNCLE: We will go get it later on, after the doctor has come.

THE FATHER: Well, we can see enough here; there is light from outside.

THE GRANDFATHER: Is it light outside?

THE FATHER: Lighter than here.

THE UNCLE: For my part, I would just as soon talk in the dark.

THE FATHER: So would I. (*Silence.*)

THE GRANDFATHER: It seems to me that the clock makes a great deal of noise!
. . .

THE ELDEST DAUGHTER: That is because we are not talking anymore, grandfather.

THE GRANDFATHER: But why are you all silent?

THE UNCLE: What do you want us to talk about?—You are really very peculiar tonight.

THE GRANDFATHER: It is very dark in the room?

THE UNCLE: It is not very light. (*Silence.*)

THE GRANDFATHER: I do not feel well, Ursula; open the window a little.

THE FATHER: Yes, child; open the window a little. I'm beginning to feel in need of air myself. (*The Daughter opens the window.*)

THE UNCLE: I really believe we have stayed shut up too long.

THE GRANDFATHER: Is the window open?

THE DAUGHTER: Yes, grandfather; it is wide open.

THE GRANDFATHER: One would not have thought it was open; there is not a sound from outside.

THE DAUGHTER: No, grandfather; there is not the slightest sound.

THE FATHER: The silence is extraordinary.

THE DAUGHTER: One could hear an angel tread.

THE UNCLE: That is why I do not like the country.

THE GRANDFATHER: I wish I could hear some sound. What time is it, Ursula?

THE DAUGHTER: It will soon be midnight, grandfather. (*The uncle begins to pace up and down the room.*)

THE GRANDFATHER: Who is that walking around like that?

THE UNCLE: It is I! It is I! Do not be afraid. I feel the need to walk about a little. (*Silence.*)—But I am going to sit down again;—I cannot see where I am going. (*Silence.*)

THE GRANDFATHER: I wish I were out of this place.

THE DAUGHTER: Where would you like to go, grandfather?

THE GRANDFATHER: I do not know where—into another room, no matter where! No matter where!

THE FATHER: Where would we go?

THE UNCLE: It is too late to go anywhere else. (*Silence. They are sitting, motionless, around the table.*)

THE GRANDFATHER: What is that I hear, Ursula?

THE DAUGHTER: Nothing, grandfather; it is the leaves falling.—Yes, it is the leaves falling on the terrace.

THE GRANDFATHER: Go and shut the window, Ursula.

THE DAUGHTER: Yes, grandfather. (*She shuts the window, comes back, and sits down.*)

THE GRANDFATHER: I am cold.(*Silence. The Three Sisters kiss each other.*) What is that I hear now?

THE FATHER: It is the three sisters kissing each other.

THE UNCLE: It seems to me they are very pale this evening. (*Silence.*)

THE GRANDFATHER: What is that I hear now?

THE DAUGHTER: Nothing, grandfather; it is the clasping of my hands. (*Silence.*)

THE GRANDFATHER: And that? . . .

THE DAUGHTER: I do not know, grandfather . . . perhaps my sisters are trembling a little? . . .

THE GRANDFATHER: I too am afraid, children.

(*A ray of moonlight penetrates through a corner of the stained glass and throws strange gleams here and there in the room. The clock strikes midnight and at the last stroke a sound is heard, very vaguely as if someone were getting up in haste.*)

THE GRANDFATHER: (*Trembling with special horror.*) Who is that who got up?

THE UNCLE: No one got up!

THE FATHER: I did not get up!

THE THREE DAUGHTERS: Nor I!—Nor I!—Nor I!

THE GRANDFATHER: Someone got up from the table!

THE UNCLE: Light the lamp! . . .

(*Cries of terror are suddenly heard from the child's room, on the right; these cries continue, with increasing horror, until the end of the scene.*)

THE FATHER: Listen! The baby!

THE UNCLE: He has never cried before!

THE FATHER: Let us go and see!

THE UNCLE: The light! The light!

(*At this moment, quick and heavy steps are heard in the room on the left.—Then a deathly silence.—They listen in mute terror, until the door of the room opens slowly;*)

the light from within is cast into the room where they are sitting, and the Sister of Mercy in her black garments appears on the threshold, and bows as she makes the sign of the cross, to announce the death of the wife. They understand, and, after a moment of hesitation and fright, silently enter the chamber of death, while the Uncle politely steps aside on the threshold to let the three girls pass. The blind man, left alone, gets up anxiously and feels his way around the table in the darkness.)

THE GRANDFATHER: Where are you going?—Where are you going?—They have left me all alone!

END

The Crystal Spider

To Jules Renard

Madame Rachilde

CHARACTERS:

Mother, 45 years old, bright eyes, tender mouth; she has a young face framed by gray hair. She wears an elegant black house dress and a white lace mantilla. Sensual voice.

Terror-Stricken, 20 years old. He is thin, almost wispy in his casual outfit made of pure white poplin. His face is ashen, his eyes have a vacant expression. His straight black hair glistens on his brow. He has regular features recalling his mother's beauty, much the way a dead man resembles his own portrait. Voice hollow and dull.

Written and published 1892
First performance: Théâtre de l'Oeuvre, Paris, February 13, 1894
with Lugné-Poe as Terror-Stricken
Translated by Daniel Gerould

A large drawing room, one of whose three windows opens on a terrace filled with honeysuckle. Very bright summer night. The moon illuminates the entire part of the stage where the characters are found. The back of the stage remains engulfed in darkness. One gets a glimpse of furniture with heavy, old-fashioned shapes. In the midst of this demi-obscurity, a tall psyche mirror in the empire style, supported on each side by slender swan necks with brass beaks. A faint reflection of light on the mirror, but, seen from the lighted terrace, this reflection seems not to come from the moon, but rather appears to emanate from the psyche itself, as though the light were intrinsic to it.

The two characters are seated in front of the open door.

MOTHER: Come now, little boy, tell me what you're thinking of?

TERROR-STRICKEN: But . . . nothing, mother.

MOTHER: (Stretching out in her armchair.) What a fragrance that honeysuckle has! Do you smell it? It makes you tipsy. You might say it's one of those delicate liqueurs of her ladyship . . . (She licks her lips.)

TERROR-STRICKEN: That honeysuckle, a liqueur? Ah! . . . Yes, mother.

MOTHER: You're not cold, I hope, in weather like this? And you don't have a headache, do you?

TERROR-STRICKEN: No, thank you, mother.

MOTHER: Thank you for what? (She leans over and looks at him closely.) My poor little Sylvius! Now admit it, it is not amusing to keep an old woman company. (Inhaling the breeze.) What a mild night! There is no need to have the lamps brought in, is there? I told François that he could go for a walk and I wager he's carrying on with the maids. We shall stay here until the moon starts down . . . (A moment of silence. She begins again in a serious tone.) Sylvius, it is no use denying it, you are unsuccessful in love. The longer you go on like this, the thinner you get . . .

TERROR-STRICKEN: I have already assured you, mother, that I have never loved any one but you!

MOTHER: (*Touched.*) What foolishness! Come now, if she is royally born, we could afford to treat ourselves to her, now couldn't we! And if she is a scullery maid, just as long as you don't marry her . . .

TERROR-STRICKEN: Mother, your teasing drives needles through my ear-drum.

MOTHER: And if you've run into debt, into serious debt, well, what of it? You know I can pay it off.

TEROR-STRICKEN: That debt again! But I have more money than I know how to spend.

MOTHER: (*Lowering her voice and drawing her chair closer.*) Now then, you won't get angry, will you Sylvius? Why, to be sure! You men have secrets that are more shameful than wicked passions or debts . . . I have made up my mind to take charge of everything . . . Do you understand what I mean? If my own flesh and blood took sick . . . well, then (*delicately*), we would look after our health until we were cured . . .

TERROR-STRICKEN: (*With a gesture of disgust.*) You have gone mad, mother.

MOTHER: (*Carried away.*) Yes, I am actually beginning to believe that I am losing my mind every time I set eyes on you. (*She gets up.*) Haven't you noticed how the sight of you inspires me with fear?

TERROR-STRICKEN: (*Trembling.*) With fear!

MOTHER: (*Coming back and leaning over him, full of caresses.*) I didn't mean to cause you pain, Sylvius! (*A pause, then she straightens up, and speaks with vehemence.*) Oh! What little slut has taken my Sylvius away from me? Because there is a slut at the bottom of this, I'm sure of that . . .

TERROR-STRICKEN: (*Shrugging his shoulders.*) Why not make it several sluts, if that's what you want to hear, mother.

MOTHER: (*Remaining on her feet and seeming to talk to herself.*) Or perhaps a dreadful vice, one of those vices of which we respectable women do not have even the slightest inkling. (*She speaks directly to him.*) Since this happened to you, I've started reading novels in an attempt to understand you, and I haven't yet discovered anything I didn't already know.

TERROR-STRICKEN: Oh! I can well imagine.

MOTHER: It's settled! Tomorrow we shall invite guests, women, young ladies. You'll see your cousin Sylvia again. There was a time when you used to follow her about like a little doggie, and now she has grown quite charming; a bit of a flirt, I grant you, but so captivating with her imitations of all the popular singers in vogue! . . . Oh! My dear, woman should be the sole pre-occupation of man. Then love makes you beautiful! (*She caresses his chin.*) You will be able to question the mirror in your dressing room! . . .

TERROR-STRICKEN: (*Starting up with a gesture of dread.*) The mirror in my dressing room! . . . Dear God! Women, young ladies, creatures who all have mirror reflections in the depths of their eyes . . . Mother! Mother! Do you want to kill me . . .

MOTHER: (*Astonished.*) What! Still harboring ideas on the subject of mirrors! So it is serious, that mania of yours? My word, he has ended up imagining he's ugly. (*She laughs.*)

TERROR-STRICKEN: (*Casting a furtive look behind him, in the direction of the psyche which the moon distantly illumines.*) Mamma, I beg you, let's drop this topic. No, my physical well-being is not at issue . . . There are psychic reasons . . . Dear God! You can see that I am stifling! . . . Won't you ever understand! Oh! It's been incessant persecution for the past week! You are crushing me! No, I'm not ill! . . . I need to be alone, that's all it is. Invite all the mirrors that you like and hang from the walls all the women on earth, but don't tickle me in order to make me laugh . . . Ah! It's more than I can stand, more than I can stand! . . . (*He sinks back into his armchair.*)

MOTHER: (*Clutching him in her arms.*) You are stifling, Sylvius, who are you saying that to? As if *I* weren't consumed with anxiety when I see that sullen look on your face! Make an effort, I am capable of understanding you, you'll see . . . since I adore you! . . . (*She kisses him.*)

TERROR-STRICKEN: (*Suddenly bursting out.*) Well, all right then! Yes, that's it, I am afraid of mirrors, have me put away if you wish! (*Moment of silence.*)

MOTHER: (*Gently.*) We'll put the mirrors away, Sylvius.

TERROR-STRICKEN: (*Holding out his hands to her.*) Forgive me, mother, I am a brute. In all likelihood, I should have spoken sooner, but it is sheer torture to think that one will be ridiculed. And this can scarcely be said in a word or two . . . (*He passes his hands over his forehead.*) Mother, what do you see when you look at yourself? (*He breathes with difficulty.*)

MOTHER: I see myself, my dear Sylvius. (*She sits down again and shakes her head.*) I see an old woman. Alas! . . .

TERROR-STRICKEN: (*Giving her a look of commiseration.*) Ah! Have you never seen anything *there* except yourself? I pity you! (*Growing animated.*) Now I have the impression that the inventor of the first mirror must have gone mad with fear in the presence of his own creation! So, for you, a woman of intelligence, there's nothing in a mirror but the simplest things? In that atmosphere of the unknown, have you never seen a host of phantoms suddenly rise up? At the threshold of those dream gates, have you never felt the magic spell of the infinite keeping you under surveillance? But a mirror is something so dreadful that I am amazed, each morning, to find you still alive, all of you women and young ladies who spend your days admiring yourselves endlessly! . . . Mother, listen to me, it is a long story, and I must go far back to uncover the cause of my hatred of mirrors, for I am one of the predestined, I was *forewarned* early in my childhood . . . I was ten years old, I was down there in the pavilion of our park, all alone, and, in view of a huge, huge mirror—which has not been there for ages—I was leafing through my school notebooks, I had a make-up assignment to write out. The enclosed room, with its drawn curtains, struck me as being like a poor man's dwelling; it was furnished with garden chairs quite eaten away by the damp, and with a table covered by a dirty cloth full of holes. The ceiling leaked, you could hear the rain beating against the half-demolished zinc roof. The only touch of luxury was suggested by that huge mirror, oh! such a huge mirror, that stood as tall as a man! Instinctively, I looked at myself. Beneath the limpidity of its glass, it was flecked with lugubrious spots. They could have been water lilies swelling on the surface of a standing pool, and further down, in a shadowy recess, there rose up indistinct forms that resembled specters moving up through the coils of their slimy hair. I remember, as I stood there staring at myself, that I had the strange sensation of plunging up to my neck into that looking-glass as though it were a muddy lake. I had been locked in, I was doing penance and thus I was compelled, like it or not, to remain immersed in that stagnant water. By dint of fixing my eyes on the eyes of my image, I made out a small dot shining in the thick of those mists, and at the same time I discerned a faint insect sound coming from the place where I saw the dot. Almost imperceptibly this dot spread out into a star. It crackled like darting streaks of lightning in the depths of that somnolent atmosphere, it buzzed the way a fly does against a window-pane. Mother! That is what I saw and heard! I was not dreaming, I was wide awake. No possible way for a ten year old to explain it, nor could a grown-up do any better, I assure you! I was aware that the pavilion had a shed attached to it where the garden tools were kept; but it was unoccupied. I told myself that, in all probability, some spider of an unknown species was about to leap at my face, and, paralyzed, I remained rooted to the spot, my arms frozen at my side. The white spider kept coming at me, it turned into a young crab with a silver shell, its head became a constellation of dazzling arcs, its claws stretched out ever closer to my reflected head, it penetrated my forehead, split my temples, devoured my pupils, slowly effaced my image, decapitated me. For a moment I saw myself standing there bolt upright, arms twisted in horror, bearing upon my shoulders a monstrous beast that had the sinister look of a cuttlefish! I tried to cry out; but, as invariably happens in nightmares, I was unable to utter a sound. From that moment on I felt myself at the mercy of the crystal spider who was sucking my brains out! And it kept on buzzing, with the dull drone of a beast who has decided to finish off its enemy once and for all . . . Then all of a sudden, the huge looking-glass shattered under the enormous pressure of the monster's tentacles, and this entire fictional vision crumbled in glittering fragments, one of which slightly cut my hand. I let out harrowing cries and fainted . . . When I was in a state to comprehend, our gardener, who had made his way into my prison to reassure me, showed me the brace and bit that he had been using, *on the other side of the wall*, with the sole intent of driving in an immense nail! In piercing the wall, he had also pierced the looking-glass, without suspecting anything, as he went about his work to the accompaniment of the grinding sound made by the tool. My wound was not serious . . . The good man was afraid that there might be a fuss . . . and I promised to keep quiet about the whole thing . . . From that day on, I have been inordinately preoccupied with mirrors, despite the nervous revulsion I felt for them. My brief existence has been deeply marked by their satanic reflections. And since the first physical contact, I have suffered many other spiritual blows . . . At one point, I am haunted by the grotesque memory of the way I looked in my schoolboy laurels. At another, I am forced to view the photographic negative of my carnal sins . . . A mystery lies at the heart of this pursuit by the mirror, this hunt for the guilty one aimed at me alone!—(He becomes lost in dreams for a moment, then begins again, growing more and more animated.) At me alone? . . . But no! Believe me, mother, those who see clearly are as terror-stricken as I am. After all, does any one know why this piece of glass that we coat with quicksilver suddenly acquires the depths of an abyss . . . and makes the world double? The mirror contains the problem of life perpetually confronting man! Does any one know precisely what Narcissus saw in the fountain or what it was that killed him? . . .

MOTHER: (Shuddering.) Oh! Sylvius! Now you terrify me. So you are not merely telling me far-fetched stories? Is it really true . . . that you think about such things?

TERROR-STRICKEN: Mother, would you dare, right at this very moment, go and look at yourself in a mirror?

MOTHER: (Turning around towards the back of the drawing room, very disturbed.) No! No! I would not dare to . . . If we lighted a lamp . . .

TERROR-STRICKEN: (Forcing her to sit down again and sneering.) There . . . I knew that you too would be afraid! In just a few moments you will see in there very clearly! Woman, why do you insist upon peopling our apartments with those cynical blunders that ensure I can never, never be alone? Why do you throw in my face this master-spy who has the power to weep my tears? One evening when I was draping a fur pelisse over your shoulders as we were leaving a ball, I saw in a mirror smiling voluptuously a lady who resembled you, mother! . . . One morning while I was waiting for my cousin Sylvia, cooling my heels at her door, a bouquet of orchids in my hand, I saw the door swing partly open on an immense looking-glass where there was reflected a beautiful naked girl in a provocative pose! . . . Mother, looking-glasses are deep pits where women's virtue and men's peace of mind founder together.

MOTHER: Shut your mouth! I do not wish to hear any more from you.

TERROR-STRICKEN: (Seizing her arm and rising to his feet.) Mother, have you ever come across those soliciting mirrors that grab you by the sleeve in the streets of great cities? Or those that drop down on you suddenly like cloudbursts? Or the mirrors in shop windows encased in frames which are disgustingly sham, as creatures for sale are enveloped in rouge and tinsel? Have you seen them offer you the resplendent flanks where each and every passer-by has slept in quick succession? Infernal mirrors! But they accost us on all sides.

They spring up from oceans, rivers, streams! By drinking out of my glass, I confirm my own hideousness. Our neighbor who thinks he has only one ulcer always has two! . . . Mirrors personify the art of the informer, and they transmute a slight annoyance into infinite despair. They lurk in the dewdrop changing the heart of a flower into a heart swollen with sobs. By turn, full of lying promises of joy or replete with secrets shameful (and sterile as prostitutes), they retain neither impress nor color. If *she* has slipped into the arms of *another* in front of the mirror which I contemplate, I always see myself in the place of *the other*! (*Furious.*) They are infamous torturers who remain insensible, and yet, endowed with Satan's power, if they saw God, mother, they would look just like him! . . .

MOTHER: (*In a suppliant tone.*) Sylvius! The moon has reached the corner of the wall. Go fetch a lamp, I want to look *in* there . . .

TERROR-STRICKEN: (*In a voice grown once again sepulchral.*) Oh! I tell you these things because you force me to! I truly lack all qualities to become the fatal voice of revelation, but it is fitting that blind women, quite by chance, discover the terrifying situation they create for men who see, even in the shadows. Sumptuously you install those relentless jailors in our quarters; for love of you we must endure them. And in return for our patience they strike us in the face with our own image, our own vileness, our own absurd gestures. Ah! Cursed be your doubles, at least this once! Cursed be our rivals! Between you and them there exist a diabolical pact. (*In a desolate tone of voice.*) Have you ever noticed, on a snowy winter morning, those birds circling above the trap that glitters and leads them to believe it is a miraculous pile of silvery oats or golden wheat? Have you seen them, as they fall, fall, one by one, from the heights of heaven, wings shattered, beak bloody, their eyes all the while still dazzled by the splendors of their delusion! There is the mirror to catch skylarks and there is the mirror to catch men, the one that lies in wait at the dangerous turn in their obscure existence, the one that will watch them die, forehead pressed against the glazed crystal of its enigma . . .

MOTHER: (*Clinging desperately to him.*) No! I can bear no more! I am already suffering too much! Your voice is killing me! Anxiety grips me by the throat! Have you no pity left for your mother, Sylvius? I wanted to know, I was wrong. Pardon me! Go fetch the lamps, I beg you! (*She goes down on her knees, clasps her hands together.*) I feel as though I am paralyzed.

TERROR-STRICKEN: (*Staggering.*) And *I* am afraid of the mirror concealed in the dark, your huge psyche-mirror, mother . . .

MOTHER: (*Exasperated.*) Coward! Don't you think I am even more terrfied than you! Will you do as I tell you or not!

TERROR-STRICKEN: (*Getting to his feet, beside himself.*) Very well, so be it! I am going to get the light for you!

(He rushes furiously in the direction of the psyche, behind which the living room door is located. For an instant, he races through a deep night . . . All of a sudden, the terrible overturning of a huge piece of furniture, the ringing sound of shattering glass and the pitiful howling of a man whose throat has been cut . . .)

END

Death and the Fool

Hugo von Hofmannsthal

CHARACTERS:

Death
Claudio, a nobleman
His Valet
Claudio's Mother ⎤
A Mistress of Claudio ⎬ Dead
A Friend of his youth ⎦

Claudio's house. Costumes of the 1820s.

Written 1893
Published 1894
First performances: Theater am Gärtner-Platz, Munich, November 13, 1898
                    Max Reinhardt's Kammerspiele, Berlin, 1908
Translated by Max Batt, revised and adapted

Claudio's study, Empire style. In the background to the left and right, large windows; in the center, glass doors opening on to the balcony, from which a suspended wooden staircase leads to the garden. On the left side, a white double door; on the right, a similar one leading to the bedroom, closed off by a green velvet curtain. By the window to the left, a writing desk, in front of it, an armchair. On the doorposts, glass cases containing antiques. Against the wall to the right is a Gothic chest carved in dark wood; above it, old-fashioned musical instruments. A painting by an Italian master, almost black with age. The wallpaper is light, almost white, adorned with stucco and gold.

CLAUDIO: (*Alone. He is sitting by the window. Light of the setting sun.*)
    The farthest mountains in a humid light
    Suffused with sun now lie in evening glow.
    Above them hover alabaster clouds,
    Far up, gold-lined, with shadows gray and dim.
    Thus did the masters of the olden days
    Paint clouds that bear the Madonna aloft.
    Across the slopes cloud-shadows blue are cast,
    The mountain shadow fills the open valley
    And turns the sheen of meadows grayish green;
    The last of sunbeams makes the summit glow.
    How near to my heart's longing have they grown
    Who there on those broad pastures dwell alone,
    Whose works, which they with their own hands have gathered,
    Reward their pleasant weariness of limb.
    The wild, the wondrous morning wind
    Runs barefoot through the fragrant heath and wakes
    Them up; the wild bees are around them too
    And God's bright burning air.
    Nature offers them their daily tasks,
    And nature is the source of all their wishes;

In interchange of strength renewed and spent
Each touch of warm enjoyment they make theirs.
Now moves the golden ball and sinks into
The greenish crystal of the far-off seas,
The last light glimmers through the distant trees,
Now red smoke breathes a wall of hazy glow
Enveloping the shore where cities lie,
Which with their naiad arms, thrust from the flood,
In tall ships gently rock their children,
A people, crafty, bold, illustrious.
They glide across the distant, wondrous heavy,
Silent waves no keel has ever cleft.
The wrath of savage seas stirs the heart within
And cures it thus of every pain and folly.
And I see sense and blessings everywhere,
And full of longing, stare across at them;
But when I turn my eyes on nearer sights,
All things grow bleak, dreary, dull and dim.
It seems as though my whole life wasted so,
With its lost joys and tears unshed, were weaving
About these streets, this house—eternally
A senseless search, a longing all confused.

(*Standing at the window.*)

See now they light their lamps and they possess
Within their narrow walls a murky world
With all the gifts of revelry and tears
And whatever else enthralls the heart.
They are to one another closely bound,
They grieve for someone who is far away;
When one of them has come to harm,
They comfort him . . . I've never learned to comfort.
In simple words they can convey
All that one needs to laugh or weep.
They need not beat with bleeding fists
Against the seven nailed-up doors.
What do I know of human life?
True, I appeared to dwell therein,
But at the most I studied it,
Could never get caught up in it,
Have never lost myself in life.
Where others take and others give,

I stood aside, no voice within I heard.
From all those loving lips I never sipped
The true, authentic draught of life,
I never have been shaken by true sorrow,
Alone and sobbing never walked the streets.
If ever once I felt an impulse, or a touch
Of nature's kindly gifts within me stir,
My ever-watchful mind, unable to forget,
Would loudly call it by its name.
Then when a thousand metaphors would come
To mind, all trust, all happiness was gone.
And sorrow too! All frayed and worn
By too much thought, and faded, blanched, dissolved.
Yet how I yearned to clasp it to my breast,
And how from pain I would have sucked delight:
It brushed me with its wing, and I grew faint,
Instead of pain discomfort took its place . . .

(*With a start.*)

It's growing dusk. I'm musing, pondering.
Oh, yes; the age has children of all sorts.
But I am weary and must go to bed.

(*The servant brings a lamp, and then goes out again.*)

Now the lamplight lets me see again
This storage-room full of dead bric-a-brac,
Through which I'd hoped to creep in stealthily,
If never I did find the open way
Into that life which I was longing for.

(*In front of the Crucifix.*)

Before your wounded feet of ivory,
O Lord upon the cross, have many lain,
They prayed that fire may gently come
Into their hearts and deeply stir;
When barren coldness came instead of flames,
With fear, remorse, and shame they died.

(*In front of an old picture.*)

You, Gioconda, from a wondrous background

Shining with the glow of enspirited limbs,
With enigmatic mouth, both sweet and bitter,
And splendor of eyelids heavy with dreams:
You have revealed to me as much of life
As I by questioning could impart to you!

(*Turning away, in front of a chest.*)

You goblets, you, at whose refreshing brim
So many lips have sipped most blissfully;
You ancient lutes at whose melodious sound
Many a heart was deeply stirred,
What would I give to have your spell enchant me,
How glad I'd be to let myself be caught!
You emblematic signs in wood and bronze,
Perplexing images, profusion of shapes,
You toads and angels, griffins, fauns,
Fantastic birds and golden fruit in wreaths,
Intoxicating, terrifying things,
You all must have been felt once in the past,
Begot by living, seething fancies,
Out of the great ocean washed ashore,
And you were caught in forms like fish in nets!
In vain have I pursued you, all in vain,
And by your charm have I been held too fast:
And as I let each of your self-willed souls,
Like your masks, become more deeply grasped,
Life, heart, and world grew veiled before my eyes,
A fluttering swarm, you held me encircled,
Harpies inexorable, devouring
At every brook the green shoot . . .
I was so lost in artificial things
The sun no longer saw but with dead eyes
And heard no more except through deadened ears:
I always dragged this enigmatic curse,
Not wholly conscious, yet not quite unconscious,
With petty suffering and joy grown stale
To live my life just like a book, of which
One half not yet, one half no more is understood,
And after that, the mind seeks out what lives—
Whatever caused me pain or gave me joy,
I felt it never signified itself,
But was foreshadowing of future life.

And hollow image of a fuller being.
And thus in suffering and in every joy,
Bewildered I have battled with mere shadows,
Consumed, but not enjoyed my every impulse,
Dreaming dimly that day would finally break.
I turned about and squarely looked at life:
Where speed serves not the runner in his race,
And courage does not help the fighter fight,
Where misfortune does not make sad, or luck gladden;
The senseless question gets a senseless answer;
A tangled dream arises from the dark threshold,
And chance is all, the hour, wind, and wave!
Thus sadly wise, with disillusioned thoughts
Maintained in languid arrogance, deep sunk
Into renunciation, without complaint,
I live my life here in these rooms, this town.
The people question me no longer now.
And find that I am rather commonplace.

(The Servant enters and sets a plate of cherries on the table, then is about to shut the balcony doors.)

CLAUDIO: Don't close those doors quite yet . . . What frightens you?
SERVANT:
Your Lordship perhaps will not believe me.

(Half to himself, frightened.)

Now they have hidden in the summer house.
CLAUDIO: Who has?
SERVANT:
Excuse me, but I do not know.
A motley band of most uncanny creatures.
CLAUDIO: Beggars?
SERVANT: I do not know.
CLAUDIO:
Then lock the door
That opens from the street into the garden,
And go to bed and leave me here in peace.
SERVANT:
That's just what frightens me. The garden door
I have already bolted. But now . . .
CLAUDIO: Well, what?

SERVANT:
>They're sitting in the garden. On the bench
>Where carved in sandstone the Apollo stands.
>A few are there in the shade by the fountain's edge,
>And one is even sitting on the Sphinx.
>He can't be seen, the yew tree blocks the view.

CLAUDIO: And are they men?

SERVANT:
>   Some are. But women too.
>Not beggar-like, only old-fashioned in dress,
>Wearing clothes as in some old engravings.
>With such a gruesome way of sitting there
>Quite still and with dead eyes staring at you
>As if they were looking into empty air.
>They are not human. May it please your Lordship,
>Be not incensed, but surely not for all
>The world would I approach them very close.
>God willing, they'll be gone tomorrow morning;
>By your gracious leave, my Lord, I now
>Will go and bolt the main door to the house
>And sprinkle holy water on the lock.
>Because such men I've never seen before,
>And eyes like those no human ever had.

CLAUDIO:
>Do as you please, and now good night.

(For a while he walks up and down lost in thought. Offstage there can be heard the plaintive and moving strains of a violin, first at a distance, then gradually coming closer, finally strong and full, as if it were coming from the next room.)

>   Music?
>And such as strangely to the soul appeals!
>Has that man's folly then upset me too?
>It seems as if I've never heard such strains
>Coming from human violins . . .

(He stands listening, turning towards the right.)

>With thrills both deep and seemingly long-sought
>All powerful it sinks into my heart;
>It seems to be an infinite regret,
>And then again infinite hope it seems,
>As if from these old, silent walls my life

Transfigured were flowing back to me.
As when a loved one or a mother comes,
Like the return of anyone long lost,
It stirs up fervent, pious thoughts anew,
And casts me back into a sea of youth:
A boy, I stood once thus in gleaming spring
And thought of soaring up into the universe,
A longing infinite beyond all bounds
Surged through me in an ominous flood!
The days of wandering came, in ecstasy
The whole world sometimes seemed to shine,
And roses glowed, and bells rang out,
Radiant and exultant with strange light:
How all things then were full of life
Within the reach of loving comprehension,
How I felt I was inspired and deeply rapt,
A living link in the great chain of life!
Then I divined, still guided by my heart,
The stream of love that nourishes all hearts,
And a contentment made my being swell,
Which scarce today would brighten up my dream.
Music, play on, continue yet for a while
And stir my soul down to its very depths:
Then may I deem my life as warm and joyful,
As now bewitched I backwards live its course:
For all the sweetest flames, blaze on blaze,
Melting what was rigid, now shoot up!
The heavy burden of knowledge, all too old
And too confused, that weighed upon my shoulders,
Is gone, touched by the sound of primal consciousness,
By these deep tones that came from childhood days.
From far away, with tolling of great bells,
A scarcely foreseen life is announced,
In forms, which are infinitely meaningful,
Simple yet strong both in taking and giving.

(The music stops almost abruptly.)

Now silent grows what has so deeply moved me,
Wherein I felt the human and divine!
He who unawares called up this wondrous world
Most likely now holds out his hat for coins,
A street musician on his nightly rounds.

(*At the window to the right.*)

> No sign of him down there. How very strange!
> Where then? I'll try the other window now . . .

(*As he goes to the door at the right, the curtain is drawn back gently, and in the door-way stands Death, the bow of his violin in one hand, the violin hanging from his belt. He looks calmly at Claudio, who draws back terrified.*)

> What senseless, nameless horror seizes me!
> Why, when your fiddle made a sound so sweet,
> Does it bring on convulsive fits to look at you?
> And grip my throat and make my hair stand up?
> Begone! You're Death. What is your business here?
> I am afraid. Begone! I cannot scream.

(*Sinking down.*)

> My stay, the breath of life, is failing me!
> Begone! Who called you? Go! Who let you in?

DEATH:
> Get up! Cast off hereditary fear!
> I am not ghastly, am no skeleton!
> Akin to Dionysus and to Venus,
> A great god of the soul now stands before you.
> When in the mild mid-summer's eve,
> A leaf descended through the golden air,
> It was my wafting breath that made you shudder,
> Which dreamlike stirs around the ripening things;
> When swelling feelings overflowed the bounds
> And filled the trembling soul with their warm flood,
> When in a sudden flash the vast and awesome
> Was revealed as being closely kindred,
> And you, submitting to the great round dance,
> Perceived the world as though it were your own:
> In every hour of truly great import
> That caused your earthly form to shudder,
> I it was that touched your soul's well-springs
> With hallowed and mysterious power.

CLAUDIO:
> Enough. I greet you, though my heart is harried.

(*Short pause.*)

But tell me now: why have you really come?

DEATH: My coming, friend, always has but one intent.

CLAUDIO:

But surely now my time has not yet come!
Look here: before the leaf glides to the ground,
It's had its fill of pleasant sap!
Not so with me: I have not lived!

DEATH: Like everyone, you've run your course!

CLAUDIO:

As meadow flowers torn from their stems
Are carried downstream by dark waters,
So the days of my youth have slipped by,
And I never knew that even *that* meant life.
Then . . . next I stood before the gates of life,
Awed by its wonders, racked by sweet longing
That they, miraculously sprung, would fly wide open
With all the majesty of thunderstorms.
It fared not thus . . . and then I stood inside,
Bereft of grace, and could not recollect
The deepest wishes of my inmost self,
Held spellbound by a curse that would not yield.
Bewildered by the dusk and as though buried alive,
Morose and inwardly distraught,
Half-hearted and my senses dulled,
Mysteriously checked in every act of wholeness,
I never felt the genuine inward glow,
Was never tossed upon the mighty waves,
Did never meet upon my way the god
With whom one wrestles till he grants his blessing.

DEATH:

To you was given what to all was given,
An earthly life, to live in earthly fashion.
A faithful spirit stirs within you all
Which bids you breathe an inner plan
Into this chaos of dead things
And bids you make your garden out of it
For useful work, and happiness and grief.
Alas for you, if I must tell you this!
One binds and then again is bound,
Attainment comes in wild, uneasy hours;
Fatigued and weeping till relieved by sleep,
Still hoping, full of longing, half despairing,
Deep sighing, but with strong desire to live . . .

Yet all, once ripe, must fall into my arms.
CLAUDIO:
    But I am not yet ripe, so leave me here.
    No longer foolishly will I lament,
    To this small clod of earth I'll gladly cling,
    For deep within me is the cry for life.
    The wildest dread now bursts the ancient curse;
    I feel that I can live—Oh, let me live!
    I feel it in this boundless urge:
    Once more my heart can cling to earthly things.
    Oh, you shall see, no longer like dumb beasts
    Or puppets will the others seem to me!
    All that is theirs shall speak unto my heart,
    I'll press into their every joy and pain.
    And faith I'll learn to know, which is the stay
    Of all in life . . . I'll so submit myself
    That good and evil will have power
    Over me and make me wild and glad.
    Then will these shadows come to life for me!
    And humans I shall find along my path,
    No longer dumb in taking and in giving,
    Be bound to others—yes!—and strongly bind.

(*As he notices Death's unmoved expression, with growing anxiety.*)

    For, look, believe me, it was not so before:
    You think that I did love, that I did hate . . .
    No, never did I grasp the essence of it.
    A mere exchange of empty words and forms!
    Look here, these letters I can show you, see,

(*He tears open a drawer and takes out of it bundles of neatly arranged old letters.*)

    They're full of oaths, endearments, and complaints;
    Think you I ever felt as much as they—
    Or felt what I in answer seemed to say?

(*He throws the bundles at Death's feet so that separate letters fall out.*)

    Now there you have all of a lover's life,
    Where only I and I alone resound,
    As I derided every sacred thing,
    And sought to thrill with every changing mood!

There! There! And all the rest is just the same:
Devoid of sense, or joy, pain, love, or hate!
DEATH:
　You fool! You arrant fool, I'll teach you now
　To honor life this once before you leave it.
　Stand over there, be silent, and look this way
　And learn that all the others from these clods
　Have sprung with deep love for their native earth,
　And you alone an empty, jingling fool.

(*Death plays a few notes on his violin as though calling someone. He is standing near the bedroom door in the foreground to the right, Claudio by the wall to the left in semi-darkness. Through the door to the right the Mother enters. She is not very old. She wears a long black velvet dress, a black velvet cap with a white ruffle, which frames her face. In her delicate pale fingers a white lace handkerchief. She enters softly through the door and moves about the room silently.*)

MOTHER:
　How many sweet, sweet sorrows I inhale
　With this air. Like the delicate dead breath
　Of lavender there's wafted hereabouts
　One half of all my life on earth:
　A mother's life, one third of which is pain,
　One third care, one third grief. What does a man
　Know of such things?

(*Near the chest.*)

　　　　　　　　The edge there still as sharp?
　He struck his forehead there once, made it bleed;
　Oh, yes, he was small then, impetuous,
　Ran wildly, could not be restrained. The window!
　I often stood there, listening in the night
　With eagerness for the sound of his steps,
　When worry would not let me stay in bed,
　When he came not and the clock struck two,
　Then three, and there was the first, faint peep of day . . .
　How often . . . Yet he never knew of this—
　And daytime too, I was so much alone.
　This hand, it waters flowers, beats dust
　From pillows, polishes the brass door knobs,
　Thus runs the day: but then the head has nothing
　To do: a dreary wheel goes round in circles,

With premonitions and oppressive dreams,
Full of mysterious feelings of anxiety,
Which must be closely fastened to the secret
Inscrutable sanctum of motherhood
And thus to all the deepest stirrings of
This world. But I no longer am allowed
To breathe the air of sweet oppression and
Painful nurture of a life gone by.
For I must go, must go . . .

(*She leaves by the middle door.*)

CLAUDIO: Mother!

DEATH: Be still!
You cannot bring her back.

CLAUDIO: Oh, mother, stay!
Just once let me with trembling lips
That always tightly pressed have kept till now
So proudly silent, let me on my knees
Before you . . . Call her! Hold her back!
She did not want to go! Did you not see?!
Why do you force her to, you thing of terror?

DEATH: Leave me what's mine. Once it was yours.

CLAUDIO: Yet never
Was felt so! Barren, all is barren! When did
I ever feel that all the roots of my being,
Were straining towards her, or that her nearness
Like the nearness of a divinity
Transfigured me miraculously and would fill me
With human longing, human joy and grief?

(*Unconcerned with his lament, Death plays the tune of an old popular song. Slowly a young girl enters; she is wearing a simple flowered dress, cross-laced shoes, a bit of veil around her neck, her head bare.*)

THE YOUNG GIRL:
But it was beautiful . . . Don't you remember?
Of course, you hurt me, hurt me, oh, so much . . .
But then, after all, what does not end in pain?
So few happy days have I ever seen,

And they were beautiful as in a dream!
The flowers at the window, oh, my flowers,
The rickety little spinet, the cupboard,
In which I used to keep your letters and
Whatever else you gave me . . . all of this
—Don't laugh at me—became so beautiful
And spoke to me with living, loving lips!
When after sultry nights the rain came down
And we stood at the window—ah, the scent
Of the wet trees!—All that is gone,
Whatever life it had has died!
And buried lies in our love's small grave.
Yet it was so beautiful, and you're to blame
It was so beautiful. And that you cast
Me then aside, heedless and cruel, like a child,

Who, tired of playing, lets his flowers fall . . .
Oh, God, I had no way to hold you fast.

(*Short pause.*)

And when your letter came, that last, vile one,
I longed to die. I do not tell you this
To torment you now. A farewell letter
I wished to write to you, not to complain,
Not grimly passionate, without wild grief;
Only so that for my love and me
Some day you might again feel a touch of yearning
And weep a bit because it was too late.
I did not write to you. Oh, no. What for?
How do I know how much of your own heart
Was in everything that filled my poor senses
With so much radiance and fever that
I walked in broad daylight as in a dream.
Good will can never make unfaithful faithful,
And tears do not awaken what is dead.
One does not die of it. Much later only
After long and lonely misery
Was I allowed to lie down and die. I prayed
I might be with you in your hour of death.
Not gruesomely, not to torment you now,
Only as when one drinks a glass of wine
And fleetingly the bouquet calls to mind
A mild pleasure somewhere long forgotten.

(She leaves; Claudio covers his face with his hands. Immediately after her departure a Man enters. He is about Claudio's age. He wears an untidy, dust-covered traveling suit. His left breast is pierced by a knife with a protruding wooden handle. He stops in the center of the stage, facing Claudio.)

THE MAN:
    You're living still, eternal dallier?
    And reading Horace still, delighting in
    Those clever, mocking, never stirring thoughts?
    With subtle words you came to me, and thrilled
    Apparently by that which moved me too . . .
    You said that I'd reminded you of things
    That slept within you secretly, as the wind
    At night sometimes speaks of a distant haven . . .
    Oh, yes, a fine Aeolian harp you were
    And the love-struck wind that made it play
    Was always another's exploited breath,
    Mine or someone else's. We were friends
    For a long time. We friends? That means: we shared
    Between us night and day conversation,
    Companionship with all the same young men,
    Flirtation with the same young woman. We shared:
    As between them slave and master share
    House, sedan, dog, dinner and whip:
    For one the house is joy, the other, prison,
    The sedan carries one, the other's shoulder
    Is galled by its carvings; the one holds hoops
    And lets his dog jump through; the other grooms him! . . .
    Sentiments that were half formed, the pearls
    Of my soul born in pain you snatched from me
    And tossed them in the air as though your toys,
    You, quick in making friends and quick in dropping them,
    I, with mute entreaties in my soul,
    Lips tightly sealed, and you unblushingly
    Touching everything, while for me the word,
    Abashed and diffident, died on the way.
    And then a woman crossed our path. And I
    Was seized, as when an illness first sets in,
    When every sense is blurred and overstrained
    From too long gazing at one goal . . .
    At such a goal, full of sweet melancholy
    And fragrance and wild luster, like lightning flashes
    Weaving out of the deep darkness . . . All that,

You saw it too, it tempted you! . . . "Oh, yes,
Because at times I'm very much like that,
The girl's slow, languid ways and cold hauteur—
It tempted me, a mind so disillusioned,
And yet so young." Now later were not those
Your very words to me? It tempted you!
To me she meant more than mere blood and brain!
And weary of the game you threw the doll
To me, when her whole image was defaced
By your surfeit, so terribly distorted,
Deprived of all her wondrous magic charm,
Her features meaningless, her living hair
Hanging dead, you flung at me a mask,
Degrading sweet and enigmatic charm
To basest nothingness by loathsome craft.
For this at last I hated you as much
As my dark bodings always hated you
And I avoided you.
                              Then my fate drove me,
Blessing me at last, a broken reed,
With but one goal and will within my heart—
Which yet despite your venomous proximity
Had not grown dead to every impulse—
Yes, for a high and noble cause my fate drove me
To bitter death on this murderous blade,
And then cast me into a roadside ditch,
Wherein I long time lay and slowly rotted
For things that you can never understand,
And threefold blessed as compared to you,
Who was indifferent to all and all to you.

(*He leaves.*)

CLAUDIO:
Yes, indifferent to all and all to me.

(*Slowly drawing himself up.*)

As on the stage a poor comedian—
He enters on his cue, speaks his part, and leaves,
Deaf and indifferent to all things else,
Unmoved even at the sound of his own voice
His hollow tones not moving anyone:

Thus have I passed across this stage of life
Without a trace of any strength or worth.
Why did this happen to me? Why, tell me, Death,
Did I need you to teach me to see life,
Not through a veil, but wide awake and whole,
Arousing something there, while passing by?
Why does a deep presentiment of things
Here on this earth possess the child's young mind,
Yet when these things assume reality
Bring only hollow echoes of remembrance?
Why does not your violin ring out for us,
Stirring up the hidden spirit world,
Which secretly our breasts accommodate,
Deep buried, sealed off from our consciousness,
As flowers lie buried under rock and stone.
Could I but be with you, where you alone
Are heard, untroubled by vain pettiness!
I can! Now grant me that which you have threatened:
My life was dead, so you, Death, be my life!
What impels me, who's ignorant of both,
That I should call you Death and call that life?
More life you can compress into one hour
Than all of life could ever hold for me;
All that is shadowy I will forget
And surrender to your miraculous powers.

(He reflects for a moment.)

These may be only dying reflections,
Called forth at last as life is ebbing out,
But never have I with all my living senses
Grasped so much, and so I call it good!
If now, extinguished, I must pass away,
My brain thus filled with this final hour,
Then may all this poor, pale life fade away:
For only as I die I feel I am.
Just as when one is dreaming, an excess
Of feelings dreamed can wake the sleeper up;
So now, in an excess of feelings, I awake,
From life's dream to the wakefulness of death.

(He falls dead at Death's feet.)

DEATH: (*As he slowly leaves, shaking his head.*)
    How strange these creatures are,
    Who what is inexplicable explain,
    What never has been written read,
    Master confusion and make it whole,
    And still find a way in the eternal dark.

(*He disappears through the middle door; his words fade away. It is quiet in the room. Through the window, one sees Death passing by outside playing the violin, behind him the Mother, also the Girl, close to them a figure resembling Claudio.*)

END

Karna and Kunti

Rabindranath Tagore

Bengali version in verse written and published 1899
Translated by the author into English prose

The Pandava Queen Kunti before marriage had a son, Karna, who, in manhood, became the commander of the Kaurava host. To hide her shame she abandoned him at birth, and a charioteer, Adhiratha, brought him up as his son.

KARNA: I am Karna, the son of the charioteer, Adhiratha, and I sit here by the bank of the holy Ganges to worship the setting sun. Tell me who you are.

KUNTI: I am the woman who first made you acquainted with that light you are worshipping.

KARNA: I do not understand: but your eyes melt my heart as the kiss of the morning sun melts the snow on a mountain-top, and your voice rouses a blind sadness within me of which the cause may well lie beyond the reach of my earliest memory. Tell me, strange woman, what mystery binds my birth to you?

KUNTI: Patience, my son. I will answer when the lids of darkness come down over the prying eyes of day. In the meanwhile, know that I am Kunti.

KARNA: Kunti! The mother of Arjuna?

KUNTI: Yes, indeed, the mother of Arjuna, your antagonist. But do not, therefore, hate me. I still remember the day of the trial of arms in Hastina when you, an unknown boy, boldly stepped into the arena, like the first ray of dawn among the stars of night. Ah! who was that unhappy woman whose eyes kissed your bare, slim body through tears that blessed you, where she sat among the women of the royal household behind the arras? Why, the mother of Arjuna! Then the Brahmin, master of arms, stepped forth and said, "No youth of mean birth may challenge Arjuna to a trial of strength." You stood speechless, like a thunder-cloud at sunset flashing with an agony of suppressed light. But who was the woman whose heart caught fire from your shame and anger, and flared up in silence? The mother of Arjuna! Praised be Duryodhana, who perceived your worth, and then and there crowned you King of Anga, thus winning the Kauravas a champion. Overwhelmed at this good fortune, Adhiratha, the charioteer, broke through the crowd; you instantly rushed to him and laid your crown at his feet amid the jeering laughter of the Pandavas and their friends. But there was one woman of the Pandava house whose heart glowed with joy at the heroic pride of such humility;—even the mother of Arjuna!

KARNA: But what brings you here alone, Mother of kings?

KUNTI: I have a boon to crave.

KARNA: Command me, and whatever manhood and my honor as a Kshatriya permit shall be offered at your feet.

KUNTI: I have come to take you.

KARNA: Where?

KUNTI: To my breast thirsting for your love, my son.

KARNA: Fortunate mother of five brave kings, where can you find place for me, a small chieftain of lowly descent?

KUNTI: Your place is before all my other sons.

KARNA: But what right have I to take it?

KUNTI: Your own God-given right to your mother's love.

KARNA: The gloom of evening spreads over the earth, silence rests on the water, and your voice leads me back to some primal world of infancy lost in twilight consciousness. However, whether this be dream, or fragment of forgotten reality, come near and place your right hand on my forehead. Rumor runs that I was deserted by my mother. Many a night she has come to me in my slumber, but when I cried, "Open your veil, show me your face!" her figure always vanished. Has this same dream come this evening while I wake? See, yonder the lamps are lighted in your sons' tents across the river; and on this side behold the tent-domes of my Kauravas, like the suspended waves of a spell-arrested storm at sea. Before the din of tomorrow's battle, in the awful hush of this field where it must be fought, why should the voice of the mother of my opponent, Arjuna, bring me a message of forgotten motherhood? And why should my name take such music from her tongue as to draw my heart out to him and his brothers?

KUNTI: Then delay not, my son, come with me!

KARNA: Yes, I will come and never ask questions, never doubt. My soul responds to your call; and the struggle for victory and fame and the rage of hatred have suddenly become untrue to me, as the delirious dream of a night in the serenity of the dawn. Tell me whither you mean to lead?

KUNTI: To the other bank of the river, where those lamps burn across the ghastly pallor of the sands.

KARNA: Am I there to find my lost mother for ever?

KUNTI: O my son!

KARNA: Then why did you banish me—a castaway uprooted from my ancestral soil, adrift in a homeless current of indignity? Why set a bottomless chasm between Arjuna and myself, turning the natural attachment of kinship to the dread attraction of hate? You remain speechless. Your shame permeates the vast darkness and sends invisible shivers through my limbs. Leave my question unanswered! Never explain to me what made you rob your son of his mother's love! Only tell me why you have come today to call me back to the ruins of a heaven wrecked by your own hands?

KUNTI: I am dogged by a curse more deadly than your reproaches: for, though surrounded by five sons, my heart shrivels like that of a woman deprived of her children. Through the great rent that yawned for my deserted first-born, all my life's pleasures have run to waste. On that accursed day when I belied my motherhood you could not utter a word; today your recreant mother implores you for generous words. Let your forgiveness burn her heart like fire and consume its sin.

KARNA: Mother, accept my tears!

KUNTI: I did not come with the hope of winning you back to my arms, but with that of restoring your rights to you. Come and receive, as a king's son, your due among your brothers.

KARNA: I am more truly the son of a charioteer, and do not covet the glory of greater parentage.

KUNTI: Be that as it may, come and win back the kingdom which is yours by right!

KARNA: Must you, who once refused me a mother's love, tempt me with a kingdom? The quick bond of kindred which you severed at its root is dead, and can never grow again. Shame were mine should I hasten to call the mother of kings mother, and abandon my mother in the charioteer's house!

KUNTI: You are great, my son! How God's punishment invisibly grows from a tiny seed to a giant life! The helpless babe disowned by his mother comes back a man through the dark maze of events to smite his brothers!

KARNA: Mother, have no fear! I know for certain that victory awaits the Pandavas. Peaceful and still though this night be, my heart is full of the music of a hopeless venture and baffled end. Ask me not to leave those who are doomed to defeat. Let the Pandavas win the throne, since they must: I remain with the desperate and forlorn. On the night of my birth you left me naked and unnamed to disgrace: leave me once again without pity to the calm expectation of defeat and death!

END

The Shadowy Waters

To Lady Gregory

William Butler Yeats

CHARACTERS:

Forgael
Aibric
Dectora
Sailors

Written from 1883
First version published 1900
First performance: Molesworth Hall, Dublin, January 14, 1904, by the Irish National Theatre Society

I walked among the seven woods of Coole,
Shan-walla, where a willow-bordered pond
Gathers the wild duck from the winter dawn;
Shady Kyle-dortha; sunnier Kyle-na-gno
Where many hundred squirrels are as happy
As though they had been hidden by green boughs
Where old age cannot find them; Pairc-na-lea,
Where hazel and ash and privet blind the paths;
Dim Pairc-na-carraig, where the wild bees fling
Their sudden fragrances on the green air;
Dim Pairc-na-tarav, where enchanted eyes
Have seen immortal, mild, proud shadows walk;
Dim Inchy wood, that hides badger and fox
And marten-cat, and borders that old wood
Wise Biddy Early called the wicked wood:
Seven odours, seven murmurs, seven woods.

I nad not eyes like those enchanted eyes,
Yet dreamed that beings happier than men
Moved round me in the shadows, and at night
My dreams were cloven by voices and by fires;
And the images I have woven in this story
Of Forgael and Dectora and the empty waters
Moved round me in the voices and the fires;
And more I may not write of, for them that cleave
The waters of sleep can make a chattering tongue
Heavy like stone, their wisdom being half silence.

How shall I name you, immortal, mild proud shadows?
I only know that all we know comes from you,
And that you come from Eden on flying feet.

Is Eden far away, or do you hide
From human thought, as hares and mice and coneys
That run before the reaping-hook and lie
In the last ridge of the barley? Do our woods
And winds and ponds cover more quiet woods,
More shining winds, more star-glimmering ponds?

Is Eden out of time and out of space?
And do you gather about us when pale light
Shining on water and fallen among leaves,
And winds blowing from flowers, and whirr of feathers
And the green quiet, have uplifted the heart?

I have made this poem for you, that men may read it
Before they read of Forgael and Dectora,
As men in the old times, before the harps began,
Poured out wine for the high invisible ones.

September 1900

The deck of a galley. The steering-oar, which comes through the bulwark, is to the left hand. One looks along the deck toward the high forecastle, which is partly hidden by a great square sail. The sail is drawn in toward the stern at the left side, and is high enough above the deck at the right side to show a little of the deck beyond and of the forecastle. Three rows of hounds, the first dark, the second red, and the third white with red ears, make a conventional pattern upon the sail. The sea is hidden in mist, and there is no light except where the moon makes a brightness in the mist.

Forgail is sleeping upon skins a few yards forward of the steering-oar. He has a silver lily embroidered over his breast. A small harp lies beside him. Aibric and two sailors stand about the steering-oar. One of the sailors is steering.

THE HELMSMAN:
    His face has never gladdened since he came
    Out of that island where the fool of the wood
    Played on his harp.
THE OTHER SAILOR:
              And I would be as sad
    But that the wind changed; for I followed him
    And heard the music in the wind, and saw
    A red hound running from a silver arrow.
    I drew my sword to fling it in a pool,—
    I have forgotten wherefore.
THE HELMSMAN:
            The red hound
    Was Forgael's courage that the music killed.
THE OTHER SAILOR:
    How many moons have died from the full moon
    When something that was bearded like a goat
    Walked on the waters and bid Forgael seek
    His heart's desire where the world dwindles out?
THE HELMSMAN: Nine moons.

THE OTHER SAILOR: And from the harping of the fool?
THE HELMSMAN: Three moons.
THE OTHER SAILOR:
    It were best to kill him, and choose out
  Another leader, and turn home again.
THE HELMSMAN:
  I had killed him long ago, but that the fool
  Gave him his harp.
THE OTHER SAILOR:
          Now that he is asleep,
  He cannot wake the god that hides in it.

(*The two sailors go nearer to Forgael and half draw their swords.*)

AIBRIC:
  And whom will you make leader? Who will make
  A path among these waves and weigh the wind?
  Not I, nor Maine there, nor Duach's son.
  Be patient yet a while; for this ninth moon,
  Being the moon of birth, may end our doubt.

(*Forgael rises. The two sailors hurry past him, and disappear beyond the sail. Forgael takes the steering-oar.*)

FORGAEL:
  So these would have killed Forgael while asleep
  Because a god has made him wise with dreams;
  And you, my Aibric, who have been a King
  And spoken in the Council, and heard tales
  That druids write on yew and apple wood,
  Are doubtful like these pullers of the oar!
AIBRIC:
  I doubt your wisdom, but do not doubt my love.
  Had I not gold and silver, and enough
  Of pasture-land and plough-land among the hills?
  And when you came, the North under your sails,
  And praised your war among the endless seas,
  Did I not follow with a score of ships?
  And now they are all gone, I follow still.
FORGAEL: But would turn home again.
AIBRIC:
        No man had doubts
  When we rowed north, singing above the oars,

And harried Alban towns, and overthrew
The women-slingers on the Narrow Bridge,
And passed the Outer Hebrides, and took
Armlets of gold or shields with golden nails
From hilly Lochlann; but our sail has passed
Even the wandering islands of the gods,
And hears the roar of the streams where, druids say,
Time and the world and all things dwindle out.

FORGAEL:
Do you remember, Aibric, how you bore
A captive woman from the Narrow Bridge,
And, though you loved her, have her up to me?

AIBRIC:
I thought she loved you, and I thought her love
Would overcome your sorrow and your dreams.
But you grew weary of her.

FORGAEL:
              When I hold
A woman in my arms, she sinks away
As though the waters had flowed up between;
And yet, there is a love that the gods give,
When Aengus and his Edaine wake from sleep
And gaze on one another through our eyes,
And turn brief longing and deceiving hope
And bodily tenderness to the soft fire
That shall burn time when times have ebbed away.
The fool foretold me I would find this love
Among those streams, or on their cloudy edge.

AIBRIC:
No man nor woman has loved otherwise
Than in brief longing and deceiving hope
And bodily tenderness; and he who longs
For happier love but finds unhappiness,
And falls among the dreams the drowsy gods
Breathe on the burnished mirror of the world
And then smooth out with ivory hands and sigh.
Forgael, seek out content, where other men
Have found delight, in the resounding oars,
In day out-living battle, on the breast
Of some mild woman, or in children's ways.

FORGAEL:
The fool that came out of the wintry wood
Taught me wise music, and gave me this old harp;

And were all dreams, it would not weigh in the hand.
AIBRIC:
    It was a fool that gave it, and may be
    Out of mere wantonness to lure a sail
    Among the waters that no pilot knows.
FORGAEL:
    I have good pilots, Aibric. When men die
    They are changed and as gray birds fly out to sea,
    And I have heard them call from wind to wind
    How all that die are borne about the world
    In the cold streams, and wake to their desire,
    It may be, before the winds of birth have waked;
    Upon clear nights they leave the upper air
    And fly among the foam.
A SAILOR: (*Running from the forecastle.*)
             Thrust down the helm,
    For I have seen a ship hid in the fog.
    Look! there she lies under a flapping sail.
FORGAEL: (*To Aibric.*)
    Give me the helm: call hither those who lie
    Upon the rowers' benches underneath,
    And bid them hide in shadow of the sail,
    Or crowd behind the bulwark, that we seem
    A trading galley in her helmsman's eyes.
(*Aibric goes toward the forecastle.*)
    It may be now that I can go my way
    And no man kill me; for some wind has blown
    A galley from the Lochlann seas; her flag
    Is folding and unfolding, and in its folds
    Her raven flutters. Rob him of his food
    Or be his food, I follow the gray wings,
    And need no more of life till the white wings
    Of Aengus's birds gleam in their apple boughs.

(*Two sailors come creeping along the right bulwark.*)

THE FOREMOST OF THE TWO SAILORS:
    It were better to pass by, because the gods
    Make galleys out of wind that change to wind
    When one has leapt on board.
THE HINDERMOST OF THE TWO SAILORS:
             No, for I have hope
    Forgael may find his heart's desire on board

And turn his galley about and bring me home.

(*Two more sailors come creeping along the right bulwark.*)

THE FOREMOST OF THE TWO SAILORS:
    I swore but yesterday if the Red God
    Would end this peaceful life that rots the bones,
    None should escape my sword: I would send all
    To mind his cows and swine by the Red Lake.
THE HINDERMOST OF THE TWO SAILORS:
    He has heard me and not you. Nine days ago
    I promised him that none should escape my sword
    But women and jugglers and players on the harp.
THE FOREMOST OF THE TWO SAILORS: He has heard me because I promised all.

(*There are sailors now along the whole bulwark and sailors in the shadow of the sail.*)

FORGAEL:
    Bend lower lest your battle-axes glimmer.
    The tide narrows between, and one old man
    Nods by the helm, and nearer to the sail
    A woman lies among embroideries.
    Near by, but in the shadow of the sail,
    A boy and girl hold one another's hands;
    Their hair mingles on some stringed instrument,
    And a string murmurs as though Time were dead
    Or a god hid them under the shadow of wings.
    Beyond the sail a man with a red crown
    Leans on his elbows, gazing at the sea.
    When you are aboard the Lochlann galley, lash
    Bulwark to bulwark, and square her sail by ours.
    Now rush upon her and find out what prey
    Best pleases you.

(*The sailors climb over the bulwarks beyond the sail. Forgael is left alone.*)

A VOICE ON THE OTHER SHIP: Armed men have come upon us.
ANOTHER VOICE: Wake all below.
A MORE DISTANT VOICE: Why have you broken our sleep?
THE FIRST VOICE: Armed men have come upon us. O! I am slain!

(*There is a sound of fighting.*)

FORGAEL:
    A gray bird has flown by. He has flown upward.
    He hovers above the mast and waits his kind;
    When all gather they will fly upon their way.
    I shall find out if I have lost my way
    Among these misty waters. Two! Now four!
    Now four together! I shall hear their words
    If I go nearer to the windward side,
    For there are sudden voices in my ears.
(*He goes to the right bulwark.*)
    Two hover there together, and one says,
    "How light we are now we are changed to birds!"
    And the other answers, "Maybe we shall find
    Our hearts' desire now that we are so light."
    And then one asks another how he died,
    And says, "A sword-blade pierced me in my sleep."
    And now they all wheel suddenly and fly
    To the other side and higher in the air.
(*He crosses over to the other bulwark.*)
    They are still waiting; and now the laggard comes,
    And she cries out, "I have fled to my beloved
    In the waste air. I will wander by his side
    Among the windy meadows of the dawn."
    They have flown away together. We are nearly
    A quarter of the heavens from our right way.

(*He goes to the steering-oar. Two sailors come from the other ship dragging a long rope, which they fasten to the mast.*)

ONE OF THE SAILORS: But will it hold while we are emptying her?
THE OTHER SAILOR: While the wind is light.
FORGAEL:
            The oar can hardly move her,
    And I must lose more time because these fools
    Believe that gold and women taken in war
    Are better than the woods where no love fades
    From its first sighs and laughter, before the sleep,
    Whose shadow is the sleep that comes with love,
    Ends all things.

(*More sailors have come from the other ship. One of them carries a crown of gold and of rubies. One of them leads Dectora, who has a rose embroidered over her breast.*)

AN OLD SAILOR: I have slain the Lochlann king.

FORGAEL:
  You have done well, because my bows are turned
  Towards a country where there are no kings.
A SAILOR: (*Laying the crown at Forgael's feet.*)
  I have brought his crown.
THE OLD SAILOR:
          And I have brought his queen.
  I would have spared her handmaid, but she caught
  This blade out of my hand and died of a sudden.
ANOTHER SAILOR:
  She offers great rewards if we turn east
  And bring her to her kingdom and her people.
FORGAEL:
  My way is west. She seems both young and shapely;
  Give her to Aibric, if he will. I wait
  For an immortal woman, as I think.

(*He goes nearer to Dectora, gazing at her.*)

THE OLD SAILOR:
  I left her living, thinking that I had found
  Your heart's desire and the end of all our trouble;
  But now I will kill her.

(*Forgael motions him away.*)

FORGAEL:
              All comes to an end.
  The harvest's in; the granary doors are shut;
  The topmost blossom on the boughs of Time
  Has blossomed, and I grow as old as Time,
  For I have all his garden wisdom.
                  O speak!
  I await your words as the blind grass awaits
  The falling blossoms, and the dead the living.
DECTORA:
  I will swear by sun and moon to pardon all
  And to give wealth of oxen and sheep to all;
  And to give you besides a hundred shields,
  A hundred swords, a hundred drinking-bowls.
A SAILOR:
  Cover your ears; for once we had moored our galley
  Beside a Lochlann wharf, and though she had sworn

By sun and moon and a hundred gods as well,
She would weave a net to take us.
ANOTHER SAILOR:
                    She might keep faith:
The gods hold watch about the words of a queen.
FORGAEL: Have the winds blown you among these empty waters?
A SAILOR:
She will answer now like any waiting woman
Because these waters make all women one.
DECTORA:
I and that mighty king a sudden blow
And evil fortune have overthrown sailed hither
Because I had hoped to come, as dreams foretold,
Where gods are brooding in a mountainous place
That murmurs with holy woods, and win their help
To conquer among the countries of the north.
I have found nothing but these empty waters:
I have turned homewards.
FORGAEL:
            In the eyes of the gods,
War-laden galleys, and armies on white roads,
And unforgotten names, and the cold stars
That have built all are dust on a moth's wing.
These are their lures, but they have set their hearts
On tears and laughter; they have lured you hither
And lured me hither, that you might be my love.
Aengus looks on you when I look: he awaits
Till his Edaine, no longer a golden fly
Among the winds, looks under your pale eyelids.
DECTORA: (To the sailors.)
Is it your will that I, who am a queen
Among the queens, and chose the mightiest
Of the twelve kings of the world to be my king,
Become a stranger's leman; and that you,
who might have flocks and herds and many thralls,
Be pullers of the oar until you die?
A SAILOR: She bids us follow her.
ANOTHER SAILOR:
                    I have grown weary
Of following Forgael's dream from wind to wind.
ANOTHER SAILOR: Give me a hundred sheep.
ANOTHER SAILOR:
                    Give me a house

Well sheltered from the winds, and fruitful fields,
And a strong galley.
DECTORA: I give you all as much.
ANOTHER SAILOR:
And will you swear never to be avenged
For those among your people that are dead?
DECTORA:
I swear it, thought I gladly would lie down
With one you have killed and die; for when I left
My foster-mother's garden in the south
I ceased to be a woman, being a queen.
ANOTHER SAILOR: And will you swear it by the sun and moon?
DECTORA: I swear it.
ANOTHER SAILOR:
     Let every man draw out his sword.
Gather about him, that the gods may not know
The hand that wounds him, because the gods are his friends.

(*Forgael has taken the harp in his hands and is leaning against the bulwark. The sailors draw their swords, and come toward him. Forgael plays slowly and faintly.*)

A SAILOR: A white bird beats his wings upon my face.
ANOTHER SAILOR: A white bird has torn me with his silver claws.
ANOTHER SAILOR: I am blind and deaf because of the white wings.
ANOTHER SAILOR: I am afraid of the harp.
ANOTHER SAILOR: O! wings on wings!
DECTORA:
He has thrown a druid dream upon the air.
Strike quickly; it will fade out when you strike.
A SAILOR: I am afraid of his low-laughing harp.

(*Forgael changes the air.*)

DECTORA: (*Looking over the bulwark in a half dream.*)
I shall be home now in a little while,
Hearing the harpers play, the pine-wood crackle,
The handmaids laugh and whisper in the door.
A SAILOR: Who said we had a skin of yellow ale?
ANOTHER SALOR: I said the ale was brown.
ANOTHER SAILOR: (*Who has gone into the other ship.*)
         I have found the ale,
I had thrown it down behind this coil of rope.
ANOTHER SAILOR: Forgael can die tomorrow. Come to the ale.

ANOTHER SAILOR: Come to the ale; for he can die tomorrow.

(*They go on to the other ship.*)

AIBRIC: (*Who lingers, looking at Dectora.*)
   She will say something in a little while,
   And I shall laugh with joy.
A VOICE ON THE OTHER SHIP:
           Come hither, Aibric,
   And tell me a love-story while I drink.
AIBRIC: Ah, well! they are calling me—they are calling me.

(*He goes forward and into the other ship.*)

FORGAEL:
   How little and reedy a sound awakes a god
   To cry his folding cry!

(*He changes the air again; Dectora leans against the bulwark as if very sleepy, and gradually sinks down on the deck.*)

DECTORA: (*As if in sleep.*)
         No, no, be silent,
   For I am certain somebody is dead.
FORGAEL:
   She has begun forgetting. When she wakes,
   The years that have gone over her from the hour
   When she dreamt first of love, shall flicker out
   And that dream only shine before her feet.
   I grew as old as Time, and she grows young
   As the ageless birds of Aengus, or the birds
   The white fool makes at morning out of foam;
   For love is a-weaving when a woman's heart
   Grows young and a man's heart grows old in a twinkling.
(*He changes the air.*)
   Her eyelids tremble and the white foam fades;
   The stars would hurl their crowns among the foam
   Were they but lifted up.
DECTORA: (*Slowly waking.*)
         The red hound is fled.
   Why did you say that I have followed him
   For these nine years? O arrow upon arrow!
   My eyes are troubled by silver arrows;

Ah, they have pierced his heart!
(*She wakes.*)
                    I have slept long;
I fought twelve battles dressed in golden armor.
I have forgot it all. How soon dreams fade!
I will drink out of the stream. The stream is gone:
Before I dropped asleep, a kingfisher
Shook the pale apple-blossom over it;
And now the waves are crying in my ears,
And a cold wind is blowing in my hair.
FORGAEL: (*Going over to her.*)
A hound that had lain hid in the red rushes
Breathed out a druid vapor, and crumbled away
The grass and the blue shadow on the stream
And the pale blossom; but I woke instead
The winds and waters to be your home for ever;
And overturned the demon with a sound
I had woven of the sleep that is in pools
Among great trees, and in the wings of owls,
And under lovers' eyelids.
(*He kneels and holds the harp toward her.*)
                    Bend your head
And lean your lips devoutly to this harp,
For he who gave it called it Aengus's harp
And said it was mightier than the sun and moon,
Or than the shivering casting-net of the stars.

(*She takes the harp in her hands and kisses it.*)

DECTORA:
O, Aengus of the herds, watch over me!
I sat beside my foster-mother, and now
I am caught in woven nets of enchantment. Look!
I have wet this braid of hair with tears while asleep.
FORGAEL: (*Standing upright again.*)
He watches over none but faithful lovers.
Edaine came out of Midher's hill, and lay
Beside young Aengus in his tower of glass,
Where time is drowned in odor-laden winds
And druid moons, and murmuring of boughs,
And sleepy boughs, and boughs where apples made
Of opal and ruby and pale chrysolite
Awake unsleeping fires; and wove seven strings,

Sweet with all music, out of his long hair,
Because her hands had been made wild by love;
When Midher's wife had changed her to a fly
He made a harp with druid apple wood
That she among her winds might know he wept;
And from that hour he has watched over none
But faithful lovers.

DECTORA: (*Half rising.*)

                Something glitters there—
There—there—by the oar.

FORGAEL: The crown of a far country.

DECTORA:

That crown was in my dreams—no, no—in a rhyme.
I know you now, beseeching hands and eyes.
I have been waiting you. A moment since
My foster-mother sang in an old rhyme
That my true-love would come in a ship of pearl
Under a silken sail and silver yard,
And bring me where the children of Aengus wind
In happy dances, under a windy moon;
But these waste waters and wind-beated sails
Are wiser witchcraft, for our peace awakes
In one another's arms.

(*He has taken her in his arms.*)

FORGAEL:

              Aengus has seen
His well-beloved through a mortal's eyes;
And she, no longer blown among the winds,
Is laughing through a mortal's eyes.

DECTORA: (*Peering out over the waters.*)

              O look!
A red-eared hound follows a hornless deer.
There! There! They have gone quickly, for already
The cloudy waters and the glimmering winds
Have covered them.

FORGAEL: Where did they vanish away?

DECTORA: Where the moon makes a cloudy light in the mist.

FORGAEL: (*Going to the steering-oar.*)

The pale hound and the deer wander for ever
Among the winds and waters; and when they pass
The mountain of the gods, the unappeasable gods

Cover their faces with their hair and weep.
They lure us to the streams where the world ends.
DECTORA: All dies among those streams.
FORGAEL:

        The fool has made
These messengers to lure men to his peace,
Where true-love wanders among the holy woods.
DECTORA:
What were true-love among the rush of his streams?
The gods weave nets, and take us in their nets,
And none knows wherefore; but the heart's desire
Is this poor body that reddens and grows pale.

(*She goes towards him.*)

FORGAEL:
The fool, who has made the wisdom that men write
Upon thin boards of yew and apple wood,
And all the wisdom that old images,
Made of dim gold, rave out in secret tombs,
Has told me that the undying send their eagles
To snatch alive out of the streams all lovers
That have gone thither to look for the loud streams,
Folding their hearts' desire to their glad hearts.
DECTORA:
The love I know is hidden in these hands
That I would mix with yours, and in this hair
That I would shed like twilight over you.
FORGAEL:
The love of all under the light of the sun
Is but brief longing, and deceiving hope,
And bodily tenderness; but love is made
Imperishable fire under the boughs
Of chrysoberyl and beryl and chrysolite,
And chrysoprase and ruby and sardonyx.
DECTORA:
Where are these boughs? Where are the holy woods
That can change love to imperishable fire?
O! I would break this net the gods have woven
Of voices and of dreams. O heart, be still!
O! why is love so crazy that it longs
To drown in its own image?

FORGAEL:
                  Even that sleep
That comes with love, comes murmuring of an hour
When earth and heaven have been folded up;
And languors that awake in mingling hands
And mingling hair fall from the fiery boughs,
To lead us to the streams where the world ends.

(*Aibric and some of the sailors come from the other ship over the bulwark beyond the sail, and gather in the dimness beyond the sail.*)

A SAILOR: They are always quarreling.
AIBRIC: Give me your swords.
A SAILOR: Eocha and Maine are always quarreling.
ANOTHER SAILOR: Ale sets them quarreling.
AIBRIC: Give me your swords.
A SAILOR:
We will not quarrel, now that all is well,
And we go home.
ANOTHER SAILOR:
            Come, Aibric; end your tale
Of golden-armed Iolan and the queen
That lives among the woods of the dark hounds.
ANOTHER SAILOR:
And tell how Mananan sacked Murias
Under the waves, and took a thousand women
When the dark hounds were loosed.
ANOTHER SAILOR: Come to the ale.

(*They go into the other ship.*)

DECTORA: (*Going toward the sail.*)
I have begun remembering my dreams.
I have commanded men in dreams. Beloved,
We will go call these sailors, and escape
The nets the gods have woven and our own hearts,
And, hurrying homeward, fall upon some land
And rule together under a canopy.
FORGAEL:
All that know love among the winds of the world
Have found it like the froth upon the ale.
DECTORA:
We will find out valleys and woods and meadows

To wander in; you have loved many women,
It may be, and have grown weary of love.
But I am new to love.

FORGAEL:

Go among these
That have known love among the winds of the world
And tell its story over their brown ale.

DECTORA: (*Going a little nearer to the sail.*)
Love was not made for darkness and the winds
That blow when heaven and earth are withering,
For love is kind and happy. O come with me!
Look on this body and this heavy hair;
A stream has told me they are beautiful.
The gods hate happiness, and weave their nets
Out of their hatred.

FORGAEL:

My beloved, farewell.
Seek Aibric on the Lochlann galley, and tell him
That Forgael has followed the grey birds alone,
And bid him to your country.

DECTORA:

I should wander
Hither and thither and say at the high noon
How many hours to daybreak, because love
Has made my feet unsteady, and blinded me.

FORGAEL:
I think that there is love in Aibric's eyes.
I know he will obey you; and if your eyes
Should look upon his eyes with love, in the end
That would be happiest. He is a king
Among high mountains, and the mountain robbers
Have called him mighty.

DECTORA:

I will follow you
Living or dying.

FORGAEL:

Bid Aibric to your country,
Or go beside him to his mountain wars.

DECTRORA: I will follow you.

FORGAEL:

I will have none of you.
My love shakes out her hair upon the streams
Where the world ends, or runs from wind to wind

And eddy to eddy. Masters of our dreams,
Why have you cloven me with a mortal love?
Pity these weeping eyes!
DECTORA: (*Going over to him and taking the crown from before his feet.*)
            I will follow you.
I have cut the rope that bound this galley to ours,
And while she fades and life withers away,
I crown you with this crown.
(*She kneels beside him and puts her arms about him.*)
            Bend lower, O king.
O flower of the branch, O bird among the leaves,
O silver fish that my two hands have taken
Out of a running stream, O morning star
Trembling in the blue heavens like a white fawn
Upon the misty border of the wood,—
Bend lower, that I may cover you with my hair,
For we will gaze upon this world no longer.

(*The harp begins to murmur of itself.*)

FORGAEL: The harp-strings have begun to cry out to the eagles.

END

Visitors

A Dramatic Epilogue in One Act

Stanisław Przybyszewski

CHARACTERS:

Adam
Bela, his wife
Pola, his sister
Visitor
Stranger
First Old Man
Second Old Man
Leader of the Dance
Visitors

The music played in the mansion throughout the drama is Saint-Saëns's Danse Macabre.

Written and published 1901
First performance: Teatr Miejski, Cracow, May 25, 1901
Translated by Daniel Gerould and Jadwiga Kosicka

The park. A moonlit night. In the background, the mansion ablaze with lights. Couples, laughing and chattering, pass back and forth through the park—now going into, now coming out of the mansion. Two Old Men appear on stage and sit down on a bench.

FIRST OLD MAN: How changeable everything is in this world! I remember this mansion in the days when the old Count was still alive. You wouldn't believe what vivacious, joyful balls used to take place here . . . But since these newcomers bought the mansion, everything has changed. I am still attached to it, simply from force of habit, but I no longer feel at ease here any more.

SECOND OLD MAN: But where did they come from?

FIRST OLD MAN: No one knows. No sooner had the Count's heirs put the mansion up for sale, than they appeared—God knows from where—and bought it, that's all.

SECOND OLD MAN: There is some mystery concealed in that mansion.

FIRST OLD MAN: (*Lost in thought.*) How joyful it used to be here! I remember the good times I had here thirty years ago—Oh, it was a different house then from what it is now . . . so different, so very different . . .

SECOND OLD MAN: Because a clear conscience, peace, and happiness prevailed here then.

FIRST OLD MAN: And now?

SECOND OLD MAN: There is some mystery lurking at the bottom of it. Some terrible mystery. I am not deceived by appearances, or by these incessant balls and all that artificial gaiety . . .

FIRST OLD MAN: What could be hidden at the bottom of it? Some sort of mysterious crime? Is that it?

SECOND OLD MAN: How should I know? Crime—hmm—everything is a crime. Man has been created for the engendering of crime.

FIRST OLD MAN: True, true, everything may prove to be a crime.

SECOND OLD MAN: Including life itself, since everyone lives at someone else's expense.

FIRST OLD MAN: (*Lost in thought.*) You marry a woman, yet you never know whether she loves you or not.

SECOND OLD MAN: A child is born, but you are incapable of bringing it up . . .

FIRST OLD MAN: Say you strangle a repulsive old miser, whose money you could use to make the whole world happy . . .

SECOND OLD MAN: Suppose you violate a law which in itself is some sort of crime . . .

FIRST OLD MAN: Oh, that's true! Everything may prove to be a crime . . .

(*After a pause.*)

SECOND OLD MAN: Let's not blame human beings—they have been created for the engendering of crime, and everything may prove to be a crime . . . Oh! Humans are so wretched, so wretched . . .

FIRST OLD MAN: And as for the new owners, they seem to be joyous, and yet such strange anxiety peers out from the depths of their eyes . . .

SECOND OLD MAN: Ha! Because such strange, strange visitors have filled their house. Especially the one who follows Adam step by step; wherever Adam goes, he's by his side . . . like an inseparable shadow . . .

FIRST OLD MAN: I feel strangely uneasy. I feel as though a terrible disaster were hanging over this house.

(*A moment of silence.*)

SECOND OLD MAN: Only let's not blame human beings. Sometimes humans are so wretched—although they may not even have committed any crime. Nature can be strangely malicious. It punishes for sins that it has itself implanted in the human heart.

FIRST OLD MAN: True, true! A moment of insane happiness takes its revenge in strange ways . . .

SECOND OLD MAN: Sometimes a man does not even know that he has committed a crime. All at once a little gash appears in his heart . . . it grows bigger and bigger with frightful speed . . . and suddenly he sees it all clearly, but only when he's already in the clutches of madness . . . And sometimes, even in a moment of happiness, a sudden recollection—a slight pang of conscience—makes itself felt . . . and this self-reproach brings on thousands of others, which grow more and more insistent . . . investigations and inquests follow . . . the most insignificant detail, the slightest wrong swells to monstrous proportions—and lo and behold! Your house becomes filled with strange visitors.

FIRST OLD MAN: True, true, the internal order of things decrees that a sort of mysterious, veiled justice . . .

SECOND OLD MAN: It was not created by human beings—men know only punishment, but justice is done by the heart itself . . .

FIRST OLD MAN: By the heart itself . . . hee, hee . . . for its own evil promptings and enticements . . .

SECOND OLD MAN: (*Laughing quietly.*) True, true, true . . .

(*Music is heard from the mansion. Couples gather; they all assemble on the terrace of the mansion.*)

LEADER OF THE DANCE: (*Clapping his hands.*) Ladies and gentlemen—the dance is about to begin!

FIRST OLD MAN: (*To the second.*) Let us go too. So that I can recall those beautiful bygone days when joy and conviviality reigned here . . .

SECOND OLD MAN: And a clear conscience . . . (*They go out.*)

(*Adam comes down the steps from the terrace of the mansion, deeply engrossed in thought. He stops for a moment and shakes his head.*)

ADAM: (*After a pause.*) A terrible visitor has taken up residence in this house . . . (*lost in thought*) . . . a terrible, terrible visitor . . .

POLA: (*Comes down the steps from the terrace, goes over to Adam, and takes him by the hand.*) Adam! Adam! My poor brother—I must leave this house of yours . . .

ADAM: (*Terrified.*) What? What? You wish to leave this house of mine?

POLA: There is no place for me here—that visitor of yours is driving me out . . .

ADAM: What? There's no place? No place for you? No, that cannot be! I shall build new mansions for you, made of marble—or crystal, if you like, or red porphyry and green syenite—I shall construct entire towns for you . . . entire towns . . . I shall raise up a whole new world for you—only stay here, stay here with me . . .

POLA: Oh, even if you built up the entire earth for my sake, there would still be no place for me. Your visitor will drive me out from everywhere . . . I no longer am of any use to you . . . this house of yours is a house of misery and fear, a house of bad conscience . . .

ADAM: Pola!

POLA: What does it matter, what does it matter—I know that something terrible has happened in this house, but I won't ask you anything; I do not wish to pick your soul to pieces—oh, God, why did you have to move into this house, Adam? What was it that brought you here?

ADAM: Love.

POLA: But you have committed a crime . . .

ADAM: What? What's that you're saying?

POLA: (*With a faint smile.*) I sensed it all from the start, and I curse this house that has killed your soul. (*A moment of silence.*) Yes! I am no longer of any use to you. Adam, do you remember our great happiness, that peaceful, quiet happiness before you moved into this house? That time on the cliffs overlooking the ocean by the shore? The sea was as soft and smooth as the palm of a beloved woman; the unearthly melody of dusk and the dying purple of the sky suffused the entire world—and the ocean disappeared, and the whole world drifted by and vanished from our sight . . .

ADAM: (*Suddenly.*) Oh, how happy I was then!

POLA: Do you remember only last year, before you moved into this ill-fated house, do you remember those white nights by the North Sea? The sun, which had just set, hid for a moment behind the sea—only to rise again at the very next instant—and long golden rays of light, which in a moment were about to flood the world with white radiance, pierced the vast crimson majesty covering the sky. Do you remember how ecstatically you drank in those strange wonders?

ADAM: I remember! I remember it only too clearly—perhaps if I had forgotten it all . . .

POLA: Then? Then?

ADAM: Then I might have been able to rid myself of this frightful visitor . . .

(*Silence.*)

POLA: Where did you meet him?

ADAM: Where did I meet him? Where did I meet him? Ha! On the path of life, my dearest sister. When I lost my footing and heedlessly, recklessly plunged headlong into this, this . . . disaster—hee, hee—it was supposed to be happiness . . . whoever loses his footing . . . you know . . . ends up with such visitors in his house . . .

POLA: Adam! What have you done?

ADAM: (*Looks at her with a faint smile, evasively.*) Where did I meet him? Well, you see, it was in a big city that he first attached himself to me. I was returning to my hotel late one night, and the way led through a dark and strangely gloomy park. And suddenly, out of nowhere as though he had sprung up from the earth, a man appeared before me, and looked at me with the sort of glance, with exactly the sort of glance that penetrates all the pores of your body, makes your heart contract, and causes cold shudders to run up and down your spine and chest. I stood there shivering and shaking, but our eyes were already interlocked, I could not tear my gaze away from his, our eyes were glued together . . . These were his only words: "From now on we shall remain together for the rest of our lives."

POLA: What crime have you committed, Adam?

ADAM: What human being is there who has never committed a crime? Not even a small one? And besides, what does it mean, big or small, when it comes to crime? The biggest crime may have such insignificant consequences that it turns out to be small, and vice versa . . . And what about you? At times don't you feel dread and anxiety that you may have unconsciously committed a crime, without even realizing it? Don't you feel dread and anxiety?

POLA: Not enough to make me run away from myself.

ADAM: You are fortunate!

POLA: You see, my life is quiet, peaceful, stable . . .

ADAM: Stable . . . yes . . . the way our life together used to be only a year ago.

POLA: Only a year ago.

ADAM: And are you happy with your husband?

POLA: I'm at peace, at peace. If that can be called happiness . . . (*Lost in thought.*) But why did you let . . . a visitor like that into your house?

ADAM: I had to, I had to! Just tell me: is there any house where such a gentleman has not paid a visit?

POLA: Frightful, frightful! (*After a pause, she points to the mansion, from which louder and louder music can be heard.*) And what about that? Doesn't it benumb you?

ADAM: What does it matter, what does it matter—at times I long to stupefy myself, but my visitor does not allow me to forget—that (*points to the mansion*)—that was for her, for my wife; a woman can be benumbed by something like that, but I never can . . .

POLA: Adam, I must leave you, a house of that sort is like the plague . . . The virus of unhappiness will stick to my clothes, and I'll carry it home.

ADAM: Yes, go away, go away—but with you goes my last bit of peace and consolation. (*Suddenly, in despair.*) Oh, if only it were possible to forget, if only it were possible to forget!

POLA: (*Profoundly discouraged, in a hollow tone of voice.*) Oh, if only it were possible to forget . . . (*After a moment.*) But couldn't you leave this house?

ADAM: And where could I run away to? Run away from oneself? Impossible!

(*Bela comes down the steps from the terrace.*)

BELA: Adam! Adam!

ADAM: What is it? Here I am.

BELA: (*Comes over to them.*) You are not behaving well. Why do you ask visitors to come here if you constantly keep running away? At every moment I have to look for you in all the nooks and corners. (*Irritated.*) And besides, you have invited strange, strange visitors.

ADAM: (*Lost in thought.*) Yes, terrible visitors have taken up residence in our house.

BELA: Why did you invite them?

ADAM: (*Significantly.*) But we both invited them, didn't we? Yes, both of us brought them into our house.

BELA: What do you mean? Both of us? What's that you're saying?

ADAM: What does it matter, what does it matter—it's only that Pola told me she's leaving us and going home.

BELA: What's that? Pola, are you leaving us? Adam, don't let her go! What will happen to us? Pola, take mercy on us; do you know what emptiness you'll leave behind you?

POLA: Alas, I know, but I have to go now, I have to—here, here, in this house of yours, I feel uneasy, and it is so quiet in my house, so sad, but peaceful, so very peaceful . . .

(*The Visitor unexpectedly appears.*)

VISITOR: (*Politely.*) But my dear hosts, the visitors are looking for you . . . They want to drink your health, Adam, why are you so out of sorts? And you, Madame, look somewhat downcast too.

ADAM: (*Nervously, to Bela.*) Go back to the ballroom and tell them that I shall be with them soon. I have a headache, I want to walk through the park for a little while more . . .

POLA: (*Hastily to the Visitor.*) Let us leave him alone for a moment—come with me . . .

VISITOR: (*Politely.*) Oh, no, I'll have a little talk with him, I can usually calm him down.

BELA: Let's go, Pola, let's go—do you hear? They're dancing, they're dancing . . .

(*They leave. Adam and the Visitor remain alone together.*)

ADAM: (*Looking at the Visitor with hatred.*) Well? Won't you leave me alone for a second? Won't you give me even a moment's peace?

VISITOR: You know that I am your inseparable companion. Do you remember that night in the darkened park?—I told you then that we'd remain together forever. It's not a pleasant task, but I have to stay with you. It is my destiny.—You see, I am your shadow. Understand?

ADAM: (*Profoundly discouraged.*) And you will never leave me?

VISITOR: Never.

ADAM: (*Forcefully.*) And what if I throw you out of my heart, if I find enough strength and courage to defend myself from you, if I become so strong that I am able to tell you: get out! What if I find someone or something to fill my soul and you have to stop dogging my footsteps and keep silent forever . . .

VISITOR: Hmm, perhaps someone else would be able to do that—but not you!

ADAM: And what if my reason gains the upper hand and I tell myself: what I have done, I had to do, it was the only way? . . .

VISITOR: To happiness?

ADAM: What difference does it make? To the precipice, to the abyss, to endless despair—but only that it had to happen.

VISITOR: Reason is strangely unreasonable in such cases.

ADAM: But suppose that I succeed?

VISITOR: Then I shall cast my shadow upon the wall. It will spread its frightful wings above you—wherever you go, those ghastly black wings—no! rather frightful arms, the fingers outspread and menacing, like Satan's claws, about to catch you—wherever you go you'll always see those frightful, insidious claws lying in wait—for the moment those arms are outstretched, waiting to strike, like . . . yes . . . like a panther ready to jump: in another second they'll squeeze you in their fiendish grip, right here! Around your throat —they'll enlace you in a fiendish embrace and choke you tighter and tighter . . .

ADAM: Until, until?

VISITOR: Until they suffocate you. (*Laughing.*) You're mine! Mine! Mine!

ADAM: (*Jumps up.*) But why am I yours?

VISITOR: (*Laughing in his face.*) Oh, how you'd like to silence it all and smother it somewhere in your heart! How can you ask me why you are mine? You are the one who knows the answer to that question best of all.

ADAM: And what if those arms never come down from the wall?

VISITOR: Hmm, then it will be still worse for you. I told you that those arms seem ready to spring like a panther lying in wait—hee, hee—in fact, those arms will slowly become transformed into a Satanic beast of prey—you will have it constantly before your very eyes—and at each and every moment you will feel that this beast of prey is about to jump at you, wrapping its front legs around your neck, and sinking its hind legs into your thighs, its jaws buried deep in your breast: it starts tearing apart and pulling to pieces, it cracks your ribs and gnaws through to your heart—hee, hee, hee—until it finally rips out your heart, your poor miserable heart dripping with blood . . .

ADAM: Stop, stop . . .

VISITOR: You know, in ancient Mexico among the Aztecs there was a custom for a human heart, freshly cut out of a man's breast, to be sacrificed to the Mother Sun . . .

ADAM: And to what Sun is my heart to be sacrificed?

VISITOR: Justice.

ADAM: Human justice?

VISITOR: There is neither human nor divine justice. There is only a certain order of things that decrees that everything has to be the way it is and not some other way—whoever violates this law has his heart condemned to death . . .

ADAM: Are you implacable?

VISITOR: I am a frightful visitor . . . Do you hear? A frightful visitor . . . (*Louder and louder music can be heard.*)

ADAM: Oh, that music, that accursed music . . .

VISITOR: Doesn't it benumb you? Doesn't it stupefy you? Just try, try—dance, get drunk, deaden your feelings with pleasure, music, dancing . . . Why are you running away from all that? Why do you constantly hide in the park and make it so difficult to find you?

ADAM: I cannot listen to that music, I cannot watch that dancing! It bites—it stings—it burns! Oh, those shadows, those sleeping shadows on the wall! I have always seen them, I have always been frightened by them. Every object would grow into that beast which has been ripping my heart out with its fangs, and tearing and biting . . .

VISITOR: Ha, ha, ha . . . (*Leans over and whispers into Adam's ear.*) It bites? Eh? It stings?

ADAM: (*Remains silent, in a daze.*)

VISITOR: Ha, ha—some kind of rats, eh? Rats? So it nibbles away with its tiny little razor-thin teeth, and it gnaws, and slashes, and crunches—is that it? Like a mole that uses its little paws to dig into hard bedrock, into parched ground—some sort of hardened shell—it had only seemed to be rock—and you know, with those little paws it loosens the soil, digs down slowly, ever so slowly, but deeper and deeper with such furious obstinacy. And then the mole can no longer be seen, all that remains visible is a small pile of earth—oh, no! rather a tiny grave which grows and grows—growing higher and higher the deeper the mole digs down—until all of a sudden a burial mound has been raised up; and at last it stops growing . . .

ADAM: What does it mean?

VISITOR: That the mole has done his job.

ADAM: And that grave?

VISITOR: At the crossroads.

ADAM: For murderers? Is that it?

VISITOR: Or for a suicide—hee, hee—why didn't you think of that before? . . . That's how you could have freed yourself from me . . . And it is so easy after all. We treat death far too seriously . . . And it could be arranged so discreetly, without any fuss or needless gossip. You want to avoid certain unpleasant things, you don't want it talked about . . . there is a solution for that too: right behind the park there's a lake—you go out rowing in a small boat, suddenly a storm comes up, or suppose the boat is half rotten, and—you sink down to the bottom just like that . . . An unfortunate accident . . . You'll be buried in sanctified ground . . . hee, hee . . . or say you're coming back from hunting: you've slung your rifle carelessly, you bump into a door—the gun goes off—well! it's an accident again . . . Or you go up into the mountains—now, this is the surest way of all—your foot slips on some moss, or a stone gives way . . They say it's a pleasant death: you go flying,

flying through the air; in just one second you experience the most beautiful moments of your life . . .

ADAM: So only death can deliver me from you?

VISITOR: (*Coldly.*) Only death!

ADAM: So only by death can I redeem myself?

VISITOR: Only by death!

ADAM: You are frightful.

VISITOR: Death is not as frightful. Death is kind . . . Why can't I be as kind as death? (*Voices are heard from the terrace; laughter and the hum of conversation.*)

LEADER OF THE DANCE: Adam! Adam! Won't you come join us now? We're drinking your health!

ADAM: I'm coming, I'm coming! (*He goes off to the mansion.*)

VISITOR: Remember! That is the only way to get free of me.

(*A long pause.*)

STRANGER: (*Appears from the other side; he stares at the windows of the mansion, then turns to the Visitor. Suddenly.*) Now is this the house in which those strange mysterious things took place?

VISITOR: Yes, this is the place.

STRANGER: (*After a short pause.*) A ball, music, dancing . . . hmm . . . it fails to benumb, it cannot deaden . . . It won't drive ghosts away, it intoxicates for an instant, and then the heart, momentarily inebriated, takes double vengeance for allowing itself to become intoxicated. For the human heart is frightful and vindictive. It won't give you any peace, it won't ever give you any peace . . . (*After a pause.*) Can I come in here? I am strangely drawn to where it's bright and cheerful, I am somehow irresistibly drawn.

VISITOR: Why shouldn't you come in? One visitor more—what difference does it make? In any case, soon this house will be filled with visitors whom the host himself has never met—and even now isn't he already entertaining strange visitors!

STRANGER: Strange visitors? (*Looks around, lost in thought.*) Oh, if only I could come in!

VISITOR: But the host has been waiting for you for such a long time. His destiny is to have this house of his filled with stranger and stranger visitors.

STRANGER: Perhaps I am mistaken, perhaps this house really is a place of peace and happiness, and you see, I have this unfortunate habit of coming in at moments of happiness and joy . . . But I cannot stand loneliness: it's as though I were being pursued by furies—I run through the streets, I wander aimlessly; frightful anxiety drives me, lashes me with a frenzied whip . . . and at such moments I'll crouch at rich men's gates—where the windows are brightly lighted, and there's the sound of music, and joyful laughter and the hum of voices, and all of a sudden I have the impression that I'm lost in a swamp—in total darkness—I don't know which way to turn—until all at once there appears a dancing flame, a will-o'-the-wisp! Oh, I'm saved. It will guide me, it will show me the right direction—and I go on and on, I sink in deeper and deeper, but keep going I must . . . Don't throw me out now —don't! You cannot throw me out—look! I'm decently dressed, I won't be out of place—all I want to do is watch the dancing, drink in the music, and dazzle my eyes with the light . . . oh! it won't deaden or benumb, but it will bring a moment of forgetfulness,—and in the houses of the rich one is still safe, relatively safe. You see, I am like a cunning animal, the humans hunt me down and have brought me to bay; obsessed by conscience, their hearts refuse to lie, and their minds have gone astray . . .

VISITOR: You are not mistaken this time—you will be most comfortable here. These are people who suffer terribly, but do not know how to benumb themselves . . .

STRANGER: Is that so? Then I'll come in. I love people who suffer—I love them . . . and . . . and in the houses of the rich, one is safe, relatively safe . . . (*Goes slowly to the mansion.*)

(*The stage remains empty for a moment. Loud music. The Visitor stares at the mansion, without moving. Suddenly the music stops, and after a moment, Adam comes out, swaying unsteadily on his feet, and goes over to the Visitor.*)

ADAM: Was it you who let him in?

VISITOR: He came in all by himself.

ADAM: Why did you let him in? Now I cannot cross the threshold of this house ever again.

VISITOR: No, not ever again.

ADAM: Is there no way out?

VISITOR: No way out.

ADAM: Not even for her?

VISITOR: For who?

ADAM: For my wife.

VISITOR: She will soon be here.

ADAM: Where is Pola?—I've been looking for her, I've been looking for her everywhere. Pola! Pola!

VISITOR: She has hidden in the most inaccessible recesses of your mansion. Usually so peaceful and quiet, she is now full of fears. Because you have strange and frightful visitors.

ADAM: How frightful!

VISITOR: Remember what I told you. It's easy to have an accident. A boat can sink by accident—your foot may slip in the mountains—there are thousands of possibilities . . . (*After a moment.*) Besides, you humans are strange. You take life so frightfully seriously. What for? It's the merest scrap of happiness, that ridiculous phantom which conceals the abyss of life for one moment, only to disclose a still deeper and more frightful chasm at the next . . . These moments of intoxication, the delusion that one lives for some purpose and because of some goal—and that one has aims in life—hee, hee—how ridiculous you all are—poor worms, balls in the hands of fate and destiny, controlled by the great veiled mysteries—and you still imagine you are at the helm . . . But I won't ever leave you, I cannot ever leave you . . . Look, your wife is coming this way . . . She too has been driven out of the house by that Stranger . . . Now I can leave you for a moment to your own reflections—in the great, decisive moments of life, I usually leave people to themselves . . . (*lost in thought for a moment*) or perhaps I'll wait for you; I'll take a walk in the park . . . Humans are so strangely faint-hearted at moments like this: all of a sudden life seems to them to be so strangely beautiful and appealing . . . I'll wait . . . No one has ever deceived me so far, no one has ever escaped me . . . (*Withdraws, meeting Bela on the way—they stare at each other for a moment.*)

BELA: You are frightful! You are accursed!

VISITOR: Not me, but life itself is frightful and accursed! (*Disappears into the park.*)

BELA: (*To Adam.*) Adam! Adam! Adam! Pola has already left—now everything is finished. I have lost all my strength—I cannot endure this torment any longer . . . Madness has crossed our threshold. Wild abandon, music, intoxication are of no help any more . . .

ADAM: So Pola has left?

BELA: She has run away from this house . . .

ADAM: From this house of bad conscience . . .

BELA: She ran away as I was trying to benumb myself in the dance.

ADAM: (*Forcefully.*) Now there is no way out.

BELA: (*Springs back.*) Let's run away.

ADAM: Where?

BELA: Anywhere—even to the ends of the earth.

ADAM: Pola told me that even if I built up the entire earth with the most costly mansions, there would still be no place for her . . .

BELA: Oh, we'll forget, we'll forget—look! my arms are strong as steel—I shall take you away in them; I'll cuddle and console you, I'll hug you so tight that we'll forget everything in that pleasure.

ADAM: No, no! That frightful, frightful visitor won't give us any peace.

BELA: Then what is left for us? What is left?

ADAM: What is left? We'll go rowing on the lake—the boat is rotten—the lake is deep . . .

BELA: Adam!

ADAM: Or we'll go up into the mountains—we'll climb to the heights, to the most dangerous peaks—my foot will slip, I'll pull you down with me and—and—we shall be free.

BELA: There is no other way out!

ADAM: There is no other way! (*Sobbing loudly, Bela throws her arms around his neck.*)

(*Pola runs in, looking around fearfully in all directions.*)

ADAM & BELA: (*Joyously.*) Pola! Pola!

POLA: Calm down—calm down . . .

BELA: (*Throwing her arms around her neck.*) Now you'll stay with us—I won't let you go.

POLA: (*Incoherently.*) I will not stay—I cannot stay. There is no happiness in my home, but I have peace—here you have the plague—it will cling to my dress and I shall bring it home to my husband. I shall infect my children with the poison . . .

BELA: Stay here with us! Stay here! . . .

POLA: No, no—I ran away, I hid, but they chased me, they're doing frightful things in there—do you hear? The music has stopped—the lights are going out—look! Do you see? The mansion is dark.

(*The mansion disappears into the darkness—there is only the moonlit night.*)

POLA: I ran to you. I had to see you once more. Oh, oh! What have you done? What crime have you committed?

ADAM: (*Harshly.*) What crime? No crime at all! Millions do the same and are happy . . .

POLA: Then what is this frightful penance for?

ADAM: What for? What for? (*Suddenly to Bela.*) Why didn't you redeem me—why didn't you give me a single moment of happiness?

BELA: Because you didn't want me to—you wouldn't let me, you hid from me, you drove me off, you taunted me with your sneers, you pushed me away —while all the time, I longed for you, I desired you . . . All you thought about was to benumb yourself, grow stupefied, become intoxicated, while our house kept filling up with more and more visitors.

ADAM: With strange visitors . . . Ha! Even the walls were covered with lurking black shadows—the black beast that was ready to spring at my throat. You see, I kept hearing screams and wailing, such frightful, heart-rending cries: like the weeping of a child to whom a great, great wrong has been done simply because he was good and loving . . . ha, ha . . . (*Suddenly to Pola.*) Go, go! This is a house of bad conscience. It is contagious.

POLA: (*Tries to throw her arms around his neck.*)

ADAM: (*Pushes her away.*) The plague is in this house—look! What a frightful house! Go!

POLA: Oh, God—there is no way out—and I loved you both so much, I thought

I could help you . . . (*Starts to leave.*)

ADAM: Too late, Pola, too late . . . (*Adam and Bela remain alone for a few moments.*)

ADAM: (*Lost in thought.*) So I'll go up into the mountains—up where the moss will slip under my feet, where a stone will give way by accident . . .

BELA: I'm afraid. I'm so young—and still so strong. I'm afraid!

ADAM: Then I shall go alone.

BELA: No, no, no! I'll go wherever you want, but I'm afraid—I'm still so young . . .

ADAM: I too am young . . .

BELA: I'll envelop you with such passionate love, I'll comfort and console you—look, I'm strong. I must go with you, but wait a bit; try once again; don't push me away from you—let's throw ourselves into the whirl of life, we'll drink it all in and revel in it . . .

ADAM: You won't chase the shadows from the walls, you won't find the mole in the ground . . . (*The Visitor slowly approaches.*)

BELA: What do you want? What do you want? Accursed creature! You are frightful!

VISITOR: It is only life that is frightful. How utterly ridiculous for people to be so attached to life! Death is kind and restful . . . And all this? This scrap of inane happiness, this illusion, this Satanic mirage! This intoxication with one's own strength and goals, this conviction that one is great and has so much to accomplish: all that is folly, the lure with which life catches humans. Death, death, it's the only way—to spit right in life's face and say: "You won't delude me!" And go meet death with great dignity and contempt!

ADAM: (*To Bela.*) Come, come! Are you going to come with me?

BELA: I'm so afraid, I'm so afraid!

ADAM: (*Softly to the Visitor.*) Woman is always afraid . . . (*dementedly*) hee, hee . . . Then I'll go alone . . . there's no help for it . . you stay—you still have life before you—you are still young and strong . . .

BELA: Adam! Adam! (*Remains as though nailed to the spot.*)

ADAM: (*Starts to leave, turns and looks at her, but says nothing.*)

VISITOR: I'll go with you. It will be easier for you that way. But now it's time, it's time . . .

END

Dream Comedy

Ramon del Valle-Inclán

Published 1905
Translated by Rosemary Shevlin Weiss

A mountain cave, overlooking the meeting point of two horse trails. A band of men arrives on horseback. An old woman appears at the mouth of the cave. Her silhouette stands out against the reddish background created by the blazing hearth fire. It is dusk and the eagles that nest in the rocky hills soar on high. The air resounds with the beating of their massive wings.

OLD WOMAN: How eagerly I've awaited you, my boys. I've kept a good fire going since yesterday so you can warm yourselves. Are you exhausted?

(The Old Woman enters the cave and the men dismount. They have olive-colored faces, and their pupils sparkle in the whites of their eyes with a strange ferocity. One of them stays behind to tend the horses while the others, their saddlebags on their shoulders, enter the cave and crouch close to the fire. They are twelve thieves and their Captain.)

OLD WOMAN: Any luck, my boys?
THE CAPTAIN: You'll see in a moment, Mother Silvia! Boys, gather the booty together so we can divide it.
OLD WOMAN: You've never been away for so long.
THE CAPTAIN: We were never so lucky before, Mother Silvia.

(Mother Silvia spreads a cloth on the stone floor near the hearth. Her eyes greedily follow the hands of the twelve men as they disappear into the bottom of their saddlebags and then emerge entangled in golden jewels that sparkle in the flickering flames.)

OLD WOMAN: I've never seen such precious jewels.
THE CAPTAIN: Nothing left in your saddlebags, Ferragut?
FERRAGUT: Nothing, Captain!
THE CAPTAIN: And yours, Galaor?
GALAOR: Nothing, Captain!

THE CAPTAIN: And yours, Fierabrás?

FIERABRAS: Nothing. . . !

THE CAPTAIN: Good. I warn you, my boys, any cheating and you'll pay with your lives. Bring me a light, Mother Silvia.

(*Mother Silvia takes down the oil lamp. The Captain examines his saddlebags, left on a fireside bench upon entering, and the thieves gather around. The bloody glare from the hearth blazes on that group of sallow and curious heads. The Captain pulls out a golden embroidered kerchief from his saddlebags and, when he unfolds it, we see that it serves as the shroud for a severed hand—a woman's hand, the fingers covered with rings, the skin white as a flower.*)

OLD WOMAN: What rings! Each one is worth a fortune. I've never seen any more rich or more beautiful. See for yourselves, my boys . . .

THE CAPTAIN: The hand is beautiful too, and its owner must have been even lovelier!

OLD WOMAN: You didn't see her?

THE CAPTAIN: No . . . Her hand appeared through some iron grillwork and I made it roll with a single blow of my yataghan. The grill was covered with jasmine. If it hadn't been for the flashing of the rings, her hand would have looked like another one of the flowers there. I was galloping by on my horse and, without even slowing down, I chopped it off. It fell into the flowers, splashing them with blood. I barely had time to scoop it up and flee . . . Oh, you can't imagine how beautiful it was!

(*The Captain remains pensive. A cloud of sadness darkens his face and the golden reflection of flames and dreams quivers in his black and violent eyes as they contemplate the fire. One of the thieves snatches the hand, which lies on the golden cloth, and tries to slip off the rings which seem encased on its rigid fingers. The Captain raises his head and flashes a terrible glance.*)

THE CAPTAIN: Let go of what you dare not touch, son of a dog. Let go of that hand which my yataghan cut off in an evil hour. If only I had gone blind the moment I first saw it! Poor white hand that soon will wither like the flowers! I'd give all my treasure to join it once more to the arm I cut it from . . .

OLD WOMAN: And perhaps you'd find an even greater treasure!

THE CAPTAIN: I'd give my life for one glimpse of that woman's face. Mother Silvia, you understand the mysteries of palmistry. Tell me who she was.

(*The Captain sighs and the thieves are silent, astonished to see two tears run down his rough cheeks. Mother Silvia takes the white hand between her witch's hands and effortlessly slips off the rings. She then rubs the stiff palm to cleanse it of the blood so that she can read its lines. The thieves are silent and attentive.*)

OLD WOMAN: From birth, this hand was destined to pluck the flower they call good fortune and strew it to the wind. It is the hand of an enchanted maiden imprisoned by a dwarf. While her jailer slept, her hand would reach out through her window bars, beckoning to passing travelers.

THE CAPTAIN: With what tender mystery it beckons still to me! . . .

OLD WOMAN: Yours were the first human eyes to see it. The power of the dwarf made the hand appear, to some, as a white dove and, to others, as one of the flowers on the grillwork.

THE CAPTAIN: Why did my eyes see the hand for what it was?

OLD WOMAN: Because she had adorned it with rings so that it would no longer be taken for a dove or flower. You passed by and, if you had not lopped the hand off with your yataghan, you would have married the enchanted maiden, who is the daughter of a king.

(*The Captain is pensive and silent. Mother Silvia, by the light of the oil lamp, counts and appraises the rings. Ferragut, Galaor, Fierabrás and the other thieves divide the booty.*)

FERRAGUT: Bring me those rings, Mother Silvia.

GALAOR: Leave them so we all can see.

FIERABRAS: What a good blow our Captain has made!

ARGILAO: What if these rings are enchanted and disappear?

SOLIMAN: If you're afraid of that, I'll buy your share.

BARBARROJA: I'll buy, trade, or gamble for it.

OLD WOMAN: They shine so brightly that they make even my wrinkled hands seem beautiful.

(*After these words there is silence. The cry of the owl is heard and they all listen. The silence lasts even when, at the mouth of the cave, a shadowy figure appears wearing penitent sackcloth and a long beard. He enters, muffled in a hood and bent over his pilgrim's staff. In the middle of the cave, he straightens himself up, pulls off his venerable beard, and throws it into the fire where it bursts into a light and airy flame. The thieves roar with laughter. The Captain turns his gaze upon them.*)

THE HERMIT: Captain, I bring you news that will not displease you.

THE CAPTAIN: Tell it quickly and go.

THE HERMIT: Before dawn, a caravan of rich merchants will pass through the mountain.

(*The thieves laugh wildly, baring their teeth in wolfish smiles. Ferragut sharpens his dagger on the hearthstone, and the Old Woman throws another log on the fire.*)

THE CAPTAIN: How many of them are there?

THE HERMIT: All the sons and grandsons of Elivan the Red.
THE CAPTAIN: And where are they going?
THE HERMIT: To far-off lands, laden with silks and brocades.

(*The Captain remains silent, contemplating the fire, and once again sinks into the haze of his dreams. A dog warily edges into the cave—one of those strays that roam along lonely paths in the moonlight. It sidles along the wall and, ears back, noses among the shadows. Now and then it raises its head and sniffs the air. Its eyes glow. It is a white and spectral dog. A cry is heard. The dog scampers off, carrying in its teeth the severed hand, flower of perfect whiteness and mystery that was lying on the golden kerchief. The thieves rush out through the mouth of the cave. The dog has disappeared into the night.*)

THE CAPTAIN: After it!
FERRAGUT: The shadows seem to have swallowed it up.
BARBARROJA: We're lucky it only got the hand. Mother Silvia had already
    slipped off the rings.
THE CAPTAIN: After it! I'll give half my treasure to the one who brings me back
    that hand. After it! Ferragut, Galaor, Solimán, scour the mountainside
    without missing a single bush. Barbarroja, Gaiferos, Cifer, cover the roads.
    Quick—to horse! Half my treasure for the one who brings me back that
    hand, half my treasure and all the rings you saw sparkling on its dead
    fingers. Quickly, quickly, to horse! Didn't you hear me? Who dares disobey
    my orders? Scour the mountainside, cover the roads, or your heads will roll.

(*The band of thieves remains immobile at the crossroads and, behind them, the saddled horses graze on the sour mountain grass. The moon shines down on this rocky, windswept place. Far off, the slow and sleepy caravan can be heard passing by. From the mouth of the cave Mother Silvia calls out.*)

OLD WOMAN: My boys, don't roam through the world in vain. You'll die old
    men, far from the beaten tracks, without ever finding the hand of the
    Princess . . . The caravan is passing by, so take advantage of the riches that
    luck has brought you.
THE CAPTAIN: Shut your mouth, evil old woman, or I'll cut your tongue out
    with my dagger.
FERRAGUT: I'll never let you.
SOLIMÁN: Nor I.
BARBARROJA: Mother Silvia is right.
GALAOR: The Captain has been bewitched by that hand he cut off.
CIFER: Nothing in the world could make me put on those rings.
GAIFEROS: If I get one when we divide the booty, I'm giving it back.
THE CAPTAIN: Shut your mouths, you sons of dogs! I'll go alone. I don't need

anyone. Stay here and wait for the hangman's rope.

(*He takes a step toward his band of men and stops short, looking at them with great scorn. The thieves wait, menacing and angry, their hands posed on their daggers. The sound of the caravan crossing through the mountain can be heard coming closer. The Captain, with a sharp cry, calls his horse, mounts it, and rides off.*)

OLD WOMAN: Wait! Hear me!
GAIFEROS: Don't call him. He won't listen.
ARGILAO: He'll never come back.
FERRAGUT: From now on, I'll be your Captain.
BARBARROJA: No, I'll be.
SOLIMÁN: Look, we could all say that.
GALAOR: We'll draw lots.
CIFER: Let the dice decide.

(*Mother Silvia spreads the golden kerchief that served as the white hand's shroud on the ground, and the thieves try their luck at dice. Meanwhile, along the moonlit road, a horseman races on and on in search of the hand of the Princess Chimera.*)

END

The Stranger

Alexander Blok

The portrait was indeed that of a wonderfully beautiful woman. She had been photographed in a black silk dress of an extremely simple and elegant cut; her hair, which looked as though it were dark brown, was arranged in a simple homely style; her eyes were dark and deep, her brow was pensive; her expression was passionate, and, as it were, disdainful. She was rather thin in the face and perhaps pale.

Dostoevsky (*The Idiot*, I, 3)

"And how did you know it was I? Where have you seen me before? But how is it? Really, it seems as though I had seen him somewhere."
"I feel as though I had seen you somewhere too."
"Where—where?"
"I feel as though I had seen your eyes somewhere . . . but that's impossible. That's nonsense . . . I've never been here before. Perhaps in a dream . . ."

Dostoevsky (*The Idiot*, I, 9)

CHARACTERS:

The Stranger
Azure
Astrologer
Poet
Customers in the tavern and Guests in the drawing room
Two Janitors

Written 1906
Published 1907
First performances: Concert reading, Religious-Philosophical Society, St. Petersburg, 1907
Literary and Artistic Circle, Moscow, February 3, 1913, Moscow
Meyerhold's Studio, St. Petersburg, April 7, 1914
Café "Pittoresque," Moscow, 1917
Translated by Daniel Gerould

The First Vision

A neighborhood tavern. There flickers a dull white light from an acetylene lamp in a battered shade. Absolutely identical ships with huge pennants are depicted on the wallpaper. Their prows cut through the azure waves. Beyond the door, which frequently opens, letting customers in, and beyond the large windows, decorated with ivy, pedestrians in fur coats and girls in shawls can be seen passing by—caught in the evening's azure snowfall.

Behind the counter, on which there has been hoisted up a keg with a gnome on it and the inscription "Mug-and-Goblet," there are two absolutely similar men: both with hanging shocks of hair and center parts, in green aprons; but the tavern keeper has moustaches that point down, and his brother, the waiter, has moustaches that point up. By one window, at a table, sits a drunken old man—the spitting image of Verlaine; by the other, a pale moustacheless man—the spitting image of Hauptmann. Several drunken groups.

Conversation in One Group

FIRST DRUNK: I paid twenty-five roubles for this fur coat. But Sashka, there's no way I'll let you have it for less than thirty.

SECOND DRUNK: (*With conviction, deeply offended.*) You're talking rot! . . . Well, did you ever . . . I'll fix you . . .

THIRD DRUNK: (*With a moustache, yells.*) Shut up! Quit that wrangling! Another bottle, my good man.

(*The waiter runs over. The gurgling of beer can be heard. Silence. A solitary customer gets up from his corner and goes over to the counter with an unsteady step. He starts to poke around in a gleaming platter containing boiled crayfish.*)

TAVERN-KEEPER: Excuse me, sir. That's not done here. You'll handle all the crayfish we've got. No one will want to eat them. (*The customer goes off muttering.*)

Conversation in Another Group

SEMINARY STUDENT: And the way she danced, I'm telling you, good old pal of mine, just like a heavenly creature. I could have easily taken her by her delicate little white hands and given her a kiss, I'm telling you, right on her pretty little lips . . .

DRINKING COMPANION: (*Roars with shrill laughter.*) Hee, hee, our little Vasinka is lost in dreams, he's turned red as a beet! But what sort of girl is that for you? What sort of girl? . . . Eh? . . . (*They all roar with shrill laughter.*)

SEMINARY STUDENT: (*Completely red.*) Good old pal of mine, I'm telling you, it's not nice to laugh at people. So then I'd have taken her and carried her away from their brazen glances, and she would have danced for me in the street, in the white snow . . . like a bird, she would have flown off. And I'd have sprouted wings, and flown after her, over the white snow . . . (*They all roar with laughter.*)

SECOND DRINKING COMPANION: Look here, Vaska, on newly fallen snow you won't fly so very fast . . .

FIRST DRINKING COMPANION: The going would be easier if you wait till the real cold sets in; otherwise you and your sweetie will land right in the mud . . .

FIRST DRINKING COMPANION: Dreamer.

SEMINARY STUDENT: (*Completely dazed.*) Oh, dear friends, you didn't study in the seminary, I'm telling you, you don't understand tender feelings. But you know, I wouldn't mind another little beer . . .

VERLAINE: (*Mutters loudly, to himself.*) To each his own. To each his own . . .

(*Hauptmann makes expressive signs to the Waiter. Enter a red-headed Man and a Girl in a shawl.*)

GIRL: (*To the Waiter.*) A bottle of porter, Misha. (*She rapidly continues the story that she was telling the Man.*) . . . But, you see, honey, she'd just gone out, and then it came to her that she'd forgotten to offer the lady of the house a beer. So back she goes, and he's already opened the chest of drawers, and he's rummaging around, he ransacked everything, he ransacked everything, he thought, "She won't be coming back soon . . ." You see, honey, she starts yelling, and you know what, honey, he puts his hand over her mouth. Well, so anyhow, the lady of the house came running up, and she starts yelling too, and she called the janitor; so then, honey, he got taken off to the police station . . . (*She quickly interrupts herself.*) Give me twenty kopecks, will you. (*The Man sullenly takes out a twenty-kopeck coin.*) Something eating you?

MAN: Drink your beer, and quit blabbing.

(*They remain silent. They drink. A Young Man runs in and joyously rushes over to Hauptmann.*)

YOUNG MAN: Kostya, friend, she's waiting at the door! . . .
HAUPTMANN: Fine. She'll walk the streets some more. Let's have a drink.
VERLAINE: (*Mutters loudly.*) And to everyone his own business. And to each his own anxiety.

(*Enter the Poet. He beckons to the Waiter.*)

POET: Can I offer you a drink?
WAITER: (*A born humorist.*) It's a great honor, sir . . . Coming from such a famous gentleman . . .

(*He dashes off for beer. The Poet takes out his notebook. Silence. The acetylene sputters. The sound of hard rolls being crunched. The Waiter brings the Poet a bottle of beer and sits down opposite him on the edge of his chair.*)

POET: Only just listen. To roam the streets, to catch bits and pieces of unknown words. Then to come here and pour out one's soul to a perfect puppet.
WAITER: A bit over my head, sir, but so refined, sir . . .

(*The Waiter tears himself away from his chair and runs off to answer the summons of a customer. The Poet writes in his notebook.*)

GIRL: (*Hums.*) Oh, how I love that girl of mine . . .
        But she returns my love with . . .

(*The Waiter comes back to the Poet.*)

POET: (*Drinks.*) To see a multitude of women's faces. Hundreds of eyes, large and deep, blue, dark, bright. Narrow as lynx eyes. Wide-open as a baby's. To love them. To desire them. A man who does not love cannot exist. You too are bound to love them.
WAITER: At your orders, sir.
POET: And from out of that blaze of glances, from out of the whirlwind of glances, there will suddenly emerge, as though it had blossomed in the falling azure snow, a single face: the uniquely beautiful image of the Stranger, beneath her thick, dark veil . . . See how the feathers in her hat sway . . . See how her slender hand, encased in her glove, holds her rustling dress . . . Look, she slowly passes by . . . slowly passes by . . . (*He drinks greedily.*)

VERLAINE: (*Mutters.*) And it all passes by. And to each his own worries.

SEMINARY STUDENT: (*With a thick tongue.*) I'm telling you, she danced like an angel from heaven, and the whole lot of you good-for-nothings aren't worth her little finger. But anyhow, let's have another drink.

DRINKING COMPANION: Dreamer. That's why you drink. And why we do too—we're all dreamers. Give me a kiss, pal. (*They hug each other.*)

SEMINARY STUDENT: And no one will ever love her the way I do. And we shall live out our sad lives in the white snow. She'll do the dancing, and I'll grind the hurdy-gurdy. And away we'll fly. To the silvery moon we'll fly. And damn it all, I tell you, dear friends, don't poke your stupid, dirty noses into this. And yet all the same, I love you very much and esteem you highly. Who from one bottle will not drink, of friendship's joys must never think. (*They all roar with laughter.*)

DRINKING COMPANION: That's the boy, Vaska! You said it! Give me a kiss, pal.

YOUNG MAN: (*To Hauptmann.*) Now that's really enough. Why make her wait so long in the freezing cold? She'll be chilled to the bone. Come on, Kostya, old boy.

HAUPTMANN: Forget it. If you indulge a woman's whims, you're finished as a man—and deserve to be kicked in the face. Let her walk the streets, while we sit here and take it easy.

(*The Young Man does what he is told. All the customers keep on drinking and become more inebriated. A Man in a tattered yellow overcoat, who has been sitting by himself, gets up and addresses the whole group.*)

MAN IN THE OVERCOAT: My dear sirs! I have here a small trinket—a really precious little miniature. (*He takes a cameo out of his pocket.*) Look here, gentlemen, if you please: on one side are depicted various emblems, and on the other, an attractive lady in a tunic seated on the terrestrial globe and above this globe she holds a scepter: "Submit," she says, "Obey"—and that's all there is to it! (*They all laugh approvingly. Several of them come over and examine the cameo.*)

POET: (*Quite drunk now.*) The eternal legend. It is She, the World-Sovereign. She wields her rod and rules the world. We are all under Her spell

MAN IN THE OVERCOAT: Pleased to serve the Russian intelligentsia. I'll sell it cheap, although it didn't come cheap, but as the saying goes, anything for a friend. I can see that you're a connoisseur. Well then, let's shake on it.

(*The Poet gives him a coin. He takes the cameo and examines it. The Man in the Overcoat returns to his place and sits down again. Conversation continues only between two customers sitting at separate tables.*)

FIRST CUSTOMER: (*Picks up a humorous newspaper.*) And now the time has come to have a laugh or two. Hey Vanya, listen to this. (*With much fanfare unfolds the paper and reads.*) "A loving couple. Husband: 'Say, dearie, drop in on Mother today and ask her . . .' " (*He roars with convulsive laughter in advance of the joke.*)

SECOND CUSTOMER: Go on, gee, that's great!

FIRST CUSTOMER: (*Continues reading.*) " '. . . and ask her . . . to give Katenka a doll . . .' " (*Laughs uproariously. Goes on reading.*) "Wife: 'What are you talking about, dearie! Katenka will soon be twenty years old.' " (*He can barely go on reading he is laughing so hard.*) " 'She doesn't need a doll, she needs a good fiancé.' " (*Thunderous laughter.*)

SECOND CUSTOMER: That's really great!

FIRST CUSTOMER: She told him all right, that's what you call it!

SECOND CUSTOMER: Those damn guys, they sure know how to write! . . .

(*Once again the solitary customer begins to poke around in the platter. He pulls out red crayfish by the claws. He holds them up for a moment and then puts them down one after the other. And once again the Tavern-Keeper drives him away.*)

POET: (*Examines the cameo.*) The eternal recurrence. Once more She will gird the terrestrial globe. And once more we are subject to Her spell. See how she twirls her flowering rod. See how she twirls me . . . and I whirl with Her . . . In the falling azure snow . . . in the falling evening snow . . .

SEMINARY STUDENT: She's dancing . . . dancing . . . I grind the hurdy-gurdy, while she dances to it . . . (*He makes drunken gestures, as though he were trying to catch something.*) No, I didn't get it . . . there, I missed it again . . . but you devils won't get it either since even I can't get it . . .

(*The walls of the tavern slowly, slowly begin to whirl. The ceiling tilts, one of its corners stretches up to infinity. The ships on the wallpaper seem to sail close together, but can never actually approach one another. Through the blurred indistinct hum of voices the Man in the Overcoat, who is now seated next to someone, shouts.*)

MAN IN THE OVERCOAT: No, sir, I am a connoisseur! I'm crazy about sharp cheese, you know, the round kind! (*He makes circular gestures.*) I forgot what it's called.

HIS INTERLOCUTOR: (*Uncertainly.*) And did you . . . actually try it?

MAN IN THE OVERCOAT: Try it? You don't think I've tried it? I've had Rochefort!

INTERLOCUTOR: (*His chair swaying beneath him.*) But you know . . . there's Luxembourg . . . it smells so strong . . . and it simply crawls, it crawls . . . (*He smacks his lips and moves his fingers.*)

MAN IN THE OVERCOAT: (*Gets up, inspired.*) Swiss cheese! . . . Yes, sir, that's what you call a cheese! (*He snaps his fingers.*)

INTERLOCUTOR: (*Blinks and has his doubts.*) Well, you won't impress me with that . . .

MAN IN THE OVERCOAT: (*Loud as a rifle shot.*) Brie!

INTERLOCUTOR: Well, that . . . that . . . you know . . .

MAN IN THE OVERCOAT: (*Threateningly.*) What do you mean, you know?

INTERLOCUTOR: (*Completely crushed.*)

(*Everything is spinning, it all seems ready to tip over at any minute. The ships on the wallpaper sail on, churning the azure waters white with foam. For a moment it appears that everything is upside down.*)

VERLAINE: (*Mutters.*) And to each his turn . . . And to all a time to go home . . .

HAUPTMANN: (*Shouts.*) She's a streetwalker, so let her walk the streets! And we'll have a drink!

GIRL: (*Sings in her Man's ear.*) Farewell, my darling . . .

SEMINARY STUDENT: The snow dances. And we too are dancing. And the hurdy-gurdy weeps. And I too am weeping. And we all are weeping.

POET: Blue snow. Whirling. Softly falling. Blue eyes. Thick veil. Slowly She passes by. The sky has come open. Appear! Appear!

(*It seems as though the whole tavern has taken a plunge somewhere. The walls fly apart. The ceiling, tilting all the way, reveals the sky—wintry, blue, cold. In the azure evening snowflakes there is disclosed—*)

The Second Vision

The same evening. The end of a street on the outskirts of town. The last houses suddenly come to an end and reveal a broad vista: a dark deserted bridge across a wide river. On either side of the bridge drowse silent ships aglow with signal lights. Beyond the bridge there stretches out an endless avenue, straight as an arrow, lined by rows of street lamps and trees white with hoar frost. Falling snow drifts through the air sparkling like stars.

ASTROLOGER: (*On the bridge.*)
    The star-filled night is all ablaze.
    Two wings alone sustain my gaze.
    But count the stars none ever may.
    Beclouded is the milky way,
    And my poor gaze grows blurred and dim . . .
    Who is that drunken bum?

(*Two Janitors drag the drunken Poet along, holding him by the arms.*)

IRATE JANITORS:
    He sits in taverns guzzling beer,

We'll make short work of him out here!
Hey, Vanka, toss him on his ear!
Hey Vaska, kick him in the rear!

(*They drag the Poet off.*)

ASTROLOGER:
I see a bright new star arise,
Of all most dazzling to the eyes.
The dark black water does not stir,
And mirrored in it is the star.
Down it falls, to earth it flies . . .
Come down to us! Come here! Come here!

(*A bright and massive star glides through the sky, slowly describing an arc. In a flash a lovely woman dressed in black, with a wide-eyed look of astonishment on her face, appears crossing the bridge. It all becomes a fairy tale—with the darkened bridge and the drowsing azure ships. The Stranger grows congealed by the railing of the bridge, still retaining her pale luster as a falling star. The snow, eternally youthful, drapes her shoulders and powders her figure. Like a statue, she waits and waits. Azure (a man as blue as she) climbs onto the bridge from the darkened avenue. He too is covered by falling snow. He too is beautiful. He wavers back and forth like a soft, blue flame.*)

AZURE:
In the gleam of winter night receding,
Turn toward me your brow.
You, snow-flakes gently breathing,
Bestow on me light snow.

(*She turns her eyes toward him.*)

STRANGER:
Eyes are stars forever dying,
That wandered from their path.
It was for you, my lightly breathing,
That on the heights I pined.

(*His azure cloak is strewn with stars of snow.*)

AZURE:
In your blueness frozen
Many a star.
In my fist of iron
A bright sword.

STRANGER:
Put down, fist of iron,
That bright sword.
In my blueness frozen
Stars uncounted.

(*Azure drowses in the pale light. A ray shines against his dark cloak, as though he were leaning on a sword.*)

AZURE:
Like dreams the centuries have passed.
I waited long for you on earth.
STRANGER:
Like flashes centuries have passed.
A star, I skimmed from space to space.
AZURE:
From on your heights you gleamed
Upon my azure cloak.
STRANGER:
You saw your image in my eyes.
At heaven do you often peer?
AZURE:
I cannot raise another glance;
My gaze is bound by you, a meteor.
STRANGER:
Can you not tell me earth-born words?
Why all in azure are you clad?
AZURE:
Too long at heaven have I looked:
That's why I've eyes and cloak of azure.
STRANGER: Who are you?
AZURE: A poet.
STRANGER: Singing what song?
AZURE: Always in your name.
STRANGER: Have you been waiting long?
AZURE: Many a century.
STRANGER: Are you dead or alive?
AZURE: I don't know.
STRANGER: Are you young?
AZURE: Beauty I have.
STRANGER:
A virgin falling star.
Longs for earth-born speech.

AZURE:
  The words I know touch mysteries,
  Ever solemn is my speech.
STRANGER: You know my name?
AZURE: I know it not—and better not to know.
STRANGER: You see my eyes?
AZURE: I see your eyes. Like stars they are.
STRANGER: My shapely figure do you see?
AZURE: Yes. Dazzling you are. (*Earth-born passion begins to awaken in Her voice.*)
STRANGER: Do you long to hold me close?
AZURE: I dare not touch your hand.
STRANGER: You may touch my lips.

(*Azure's cloak undulates and disappears beneath the falling snowflakes.*)

STRANGER: Do you know passion?
AZURE: (*Softly.*) My blood has not yet spoken out.
STRANGER: Do you know wine?
AZURE: (*Still more softly.*) The elixir of stars is sweeter than wine.
STRANGER:
  Do you love me?
(*Azure is silent.*)
  Within me blood begins to sing.
(*Silence.*)
  The heart is filled with venom.
  Shapelier than all your maidens I am.
  Lovelier than your ladies I am.
  Lustier than your brides I am.
(*Azure drowses, covered from head to foot with falling snow.*)
  How sweet your life on earth must be!

(*There is no more Azure. A bluish pillar of snow has spun around and around, and then on that spot there appears to be no one at all. But a Gentleman passing by the beautiful Stranger tips his derby.*)

GENTLEMAN:
  With someone were you talking now?
  But here there's no one to be seen
  Adorable your voice did sound
  Through the empty space . . .
STRANGER: Where has he gone?
GENTLEMAN:
  Oh, yes, no doubt about it, you

Were waiting here for someone now!
Forgive a question that's indiscreet . . .
Who was that unseen friend of yours?
STRANGER: Beautiful he was. In an azure cloak.
GENTLEMAN:
  Oh, women and their romantic souls!
  Even on the street you see
  Men clad in azure cloaks!
  But what was his name?
STRANGER: Poet was the name he gave.
GENTLEMAN:
  Poet! I too am a poet!
  At the very least, when I gaze
  Into your lovely eyes,
  I could sing you a ditty:
  "Oh, you really are so pretty!"
STRANGER: Would you like to love me?

GENTLEMAN: Oh, sure! I'm not at all adverse.
STRANGER: And can you take me in your arms?
GENTLEMAN:
  I'd like to know the reason why
  I couldn't take you in my arms?
STRANGER:
  And my lips lightly grazing,
  Will you love me and caress me?
GENTLEMAN:
  My beauty, let's be on our way!
  "I'll carry out your every wish,"
  As that old-timer Shakespeare said . . .
  Now you will see that even I
  Am not deaf to poetry!

(*The beautiful Stranger submissively offers him her arm.*)

GENTLEMAN: What's your name?
STRANGER:
              Just wait a bit.
  Now let me think. In heaven, among the stars,
  I had no name at all . . .
  But here, on this blue earth,
  "Maria" is the name I like . . .
  Call me "Maria."
GENTLEMAN:
  As you wish, my little beauty.

The only thing I need to know
Is what to whisper in your ear at night.

(He leads off the Stranger, who holds his arm. The azure snow covers their tracks. The Astrologer again appears on the bridge. His mood is melancholy. He extends his arms to the heavens. He gazes upwards.)

ASTROLOGER:
    The loveliest of stars is gone!
    Empty is the blue abyss!
    I have lost the rhythm
    Of my astral songs!
    The jangling music of the spheres
    Hereafter grates upon my ears!
    Today in my high tower
    In a sorrowful hand I shall inscribe
    In my long scrolls
    News of the fall of the brightest star . . .
    And softly I shall call her
    By a distant name,
    A name caressing to the ear:
    "Maria" will be her name.
    In yellow scrolls
    These words will be set down
    By my sole hand:
    "Maria, a star, has fallen.
    She'll look no more into my eyes.
    The astrologer was left alone."

(He weeps softly. The Poet climbs the bridge from the avenue.)

POET:
    By all that's holy I implore you!
    By your anguish!
    By your betrothed, if
    Bride you have!
    Tell me, hereabouts was there
    A slender woman dressed in black?
ASTROLOGER:
    Crass common-folk! Leave me alone
    No woman have I seen here since
    My star has fallen.
POET:
    Your sorrow I quite understand.

Like you, I am a man alone.
And you, like me, must be a poet.
You did not see by any chance
A Stranger in the azure snows?

ASTROLOGER:

I don't remember. Many went by here.
And most aggrieved I am
That yours I could not recognize.

POET:

Oh, had you but seen her once,
You would have forgotten about your star!

ASTROLOGER:

It's not for you to talk of stars;
You are far too scatterbrained.
And I should like to ask you not
To poke your nose in my profession.

POET:

All your insults I shall bear!
Believe me, I am mortified
Not one bit less than you are . . .
Oh, had I not been drunk just then,
I should have followed after her!
But those two were dragging me away,
When first I noticed she was there . . .
Then down I fell into a snow-drift,
Swearing loudly, they departed,
After they resolved to dump me . . .
I don't recall how long I slept . . .
On waking I remembered that the snow
Had covered up her slender tracks!

ASTROLOGER:

I dimly now can call to mind
The sorry state that you were in;
At all events, they took you off,
And showered you with blows and kicks,
You'd grown unsteady on your feet . . .
Then I recall as in a dream,
A lady came across the bridge,
And toward her an azure gentleman . . .

POET: Oh, no! . . . An azure gentleman . . .

ASTROLOGER:

Of what they talked I do not know.
At them I looked no longer.

Then off they went, or so it seemed . . .
I was so busy with my own . . .
POET:
   And their traces were covered by snow . . .
   I'll never meet with Her again!
   Encounters such as that
   Occur no more than once in life . . .

(*They both weep in the falling azure snow.*)

ASTROLOGER:
   Is it worth weeping over that?
   My grief goes deeper yet than yours:
   My astral rhythm have I lost!
POET:
   The rhythm of my soul I lost.
   That's more important, I should hope!
ASTROLOGER:
   In my scrolls sorrow will these words inscribe:
   "A star called Maria has fallen!"
POET:
   Most beautiful of names: "Maria!"
   I'll write this in my poetry:
   "Maria, where have you gone?
   I do not see the dawn."
ASTROLOGER:
   Well now, your grief will pass!
   You've only to compose
   Poems as lengthy as you can!
   What cause to weep will you have then?
POET:
   And you, my learned astrologer,
   Have but to set down in your scrolls,
   For benefit of students, this:
   "Maria, a star has fallen!"

(*They both mourn in the falling azure snow. Slowly they dissolve in it. And the snow mourns too. It has sprinkled with its powder both the bridge and the ships. It has erected white walls on the outline of the trees, along the exteriors of the houses, on the telegraph wires. And in the distance both the ground and the river are piled high with white walls so that everything has grown white except for the signal lights on the ships and the lighted windows of the houses. The walls of snow grow thicker and thicker. They seem to have drawn close together. Gradually there is disclosed—*)

The Third Vision

A large drawing room with white walls, on which electric lights are burning brightly. The door to the hall is open. A tinkling bell frequently announces the arrival of guests. The members of the family and their guests are already sitting on sofas, armchairs, and straight-back chairs; the lady of the house is an elderly matron who holds herself as stiff as a ramrod; in front of her she has a basket with biscuits, a vase filled with fruit, and a teapot containing steaming-hot tea; opposite there sits a deaf old gentleman with a stupid face who continually chews and slurps. Young people in impeccable evening clothes either talk wtih different ladies, or herd together in corners. An indistinct hum of heedless chatter.

The master of the house greets the guests in the hall and to each and every one he exclaims over and over again in a wooden voice: "Ah—ah—ah!" and then utters inanities. At the present moment he is so engaged.

HOST: (*In the hall.*) Ah—ah—ah! Well, good gracious, now aren't you all bundled up!

GUEST VOICE: It's cold enough, I should hope to tell you! Even in this fur coat I was just about frozen.

(The Guest blows his nose. As the conversation in the drawing room for some reason or other has died down, the host can be heard saying confidentially to the Guest:)

HOST: And where did you have it made?

GUEST: At Chevalier's.

(The tails of the Host's frock-coat stick out from behind the door. The Host is examining the fur coat.)

HOST: And how much did you pay for it?

GUEST: A thousand.

(The Hostess, trying to change the subject of the conversation, exclaims.)

HOSTESS: Cher Ivan Pavlovich! Come here this minute! You've been eagerly awaited! Here's Arkadii Romanovich—he's promised to sing for us today!

(Arkadii Romanovich, coming over to the Hostess, makes various gestures designed to show that he does not have a high opinion of his own talents. The Hostess, likewise by gestures, tries to show him that the contrary is true.)

YOUNG MAN CALLED GEORGES: Misha, that Serpantini of yours made a complete fool of herself. You have to be totally shameless to dance the way she did yesterday.

YOUNG MAN CALLED MISHA: Georges (*pronounced as a French name*), you don't understand the first thing about it! I was completely enamored. It's something for the select few. Just remember she has an absolutely classical figure—what hands, what legs . . .

GEORGES: I went there expressly to revel in art. Legs I can look at to my heart's content elsewhere.

HOSTESS: What are you talking about over there, Georgii Nikolaevich? Oh, about Serpantini! What a horror, don't you think? In the first place, to interpret music—that in itself is the height of impudence. I love music so passionately and not for anything, not for anything in the world will I allow it to be desecrated. Then to dance without a costume—that's . . . that's I don't know what! I snatched my daughter out of there as fast as I could.

GEORGES: I totally agree with you. But here is Mikhail Ivanovich who is of a different opinion . . .

HOSTESS: How can you, Mikhail Ivanovich! In my view, there can't be any two opinions about it! I understand, young people have their own special fads, but at a public recital . . . when they express Bach with their legs . . . I am a musician myself . . . I love music passionately . . . All the same . . .

(*The Old Gentleman sitting opposite the Hostess simply and unexpectedly blurts out.*)

OLD GENTLEMAN: House of ill repute.

(*He continues slurping tea and munching biscuits. The hostess blushes and turns to one of the matrons.*)

MISHA: Oh, Georges, none of you understands a single thing! Is it really an interpretation of music? Serpantini herself is the perfect incarnation of music. She floats on waves of sound, and it seems that you float along with her. Now really, the body, its lines, its harmonious movements—don't they in and of themselves sing like musical sounds? No one who has an authentic feeling for music could possibly be offended by her. All of you have too abstract a relationship to music . . .

GEORGES: Dreamer! He's started the machine going. You construct some kind of theory and you hear nothing and you see nothing that goes counter to it. I'm not even talking about music, and when you come right down to it, it's of no real interest to me. And I'd be very glad to see all that at a private club. But you must admit that it wasn't announced on the poster that Serpantini would appear draped only in a bit of old cloth—that put everyone in an extremely awkward situation. If I had known, I wouldn't have taken my fiancée. (*Misha absent-mindedly pokes around in the basket with the biscuits.*) Listen, leave the biscuits alone. That's really disgusting; who's going to want to eat them if you handle them all. See how the pretty little cousin is looking at you. It's all because you're absent-minded. Oh, what dreamers. (*Misha, mumbling disconcertedly, withdraws to a corner.*)

OLD GENTLEMAN: (*Suddenly, to the Hostess.*) Nina! Sit still. Your dress is coming unhooked in the back.

HOSTESS: (*Turning red.*) Now that will do, Uncle, not in front of everyone! You're too . . . blunt . . .

(*She tries to hook up her dress without being noticed. A Young Lady comes charging into the room, followed by a colossal red-headed Gentleman.*)

LADY: Oh, how do you do, how do you do! Now I'd like you to meet my fiancé.

RED-HEADED GENTLEMAN: Pleased to meet you. (*Sullenly withdraws to a corner.*)

LADY: Please, don't pay any attention to him. He's very shy. Oh, just imagine, what a thing to happen! . . .

(*She hurriedly drinks her tea and in a whisper tells the Hostess something spicy, judging by the way they squirm on the sofa and giggle.*)

LADY: (*Suddenly turns to her fiancé.*) Got my handkerchief? (*The fiancé sullenly pulls out her handkerchief.*) Something eating you?

RED-HEADED GENTLEMAN: (*Unexpectedly sullen.*) Drink your tea, and quit blabbing.

(*They remain silent. They drink. A Young Man runs in and joyously dashes over to another gentleman. It is easy to recognize in the latter the one who led off the beautiful Stranger.*)

YOUNG MAN: Kostya, friend, she's waiting at the door . . .

(*He stumbles over the last words. Everything becomes preternaturally strange. It is as though they all had suddenly remembered that somewhere before they had uttered the very same words in the very same order. Mikhail Ivanovich, with a strange look in his eyes, stares at the Poet, who enters at this exact moment. The Poet, visibly pale, makes a general bow on the threshold of the hushed drawing room.*)

HOSTESS: (*With a strained expression on her face.*) We've been eagerly awaiting your arrival. I do hope you'll read us something. We're having the strangest evening! Our quiet little discussion is flagging badly.

OLD GENTLEMAN: (*Blurts out.*) Just as though someone had died. And given up his soul to God.

HOSTESS: Oh, Uncle, stop! You'll end up by scaring everyone away . . . Ladies and gentlemen! Shall we bring our conversation back to life? . . . (*To the*

Poet.) You'll read us something, won't you?

POET: With pleasure . . . if it will help fill up . . .

HOSTESS: Ladies and gentlemen! Quiet! Our marvelous poet will read us one of his marvelous poems, and I do hope that it will be about the beautiful lady again . . .

(*They all grow quiet. The Poet stands by the wall, directly opposite the door to the hall, and recites.*)

POET:

From flagstones melted were the snows,
Roof-tops, bare once more, began to gleam,
When in the cathedral, in a darkened niche,
Her pearls sparkled, row on row.
And from the icon, with its tender roses,
Slowly, slowly She descended . . .

(*The tinkling bell rings in the hall. The Hostess imploringly claps her hands in the direction of the Poet. He stops his reading. Everyone peers with intense curiosity into the hall.*)

HOST: Coming. Please excuse me.

(*He goes out into the hall, but once there does not exclaim: "Ah—ah—ah!" Silence.*)

HOST'S VOICE: What can I do for you?

(*A woman's voice answers something. The Host appears on the threshold.*)

HOST: Ninochka, there's a lady here. I can't make out what it's all about. Probably for you. Excuse me, ladies and gentlemen, excuse me . . .

(*He smiles embarrassedly in all directions. The Hostess goes out into the hall and shuts the door after her. The guests whisper among themselves.*)

YOUNG MAN: (*In the corner.*) Now that couldn't be . . . could it . . .

SECOND YOUNG MAN: (*Concealed behind him.*) Yes, I asure you . . . What a scandal! . . . I heard her voice . . .

(*The Poet stands motionless opposite the door. The door opens. The Hostess leads in the Stranger.*)

HOSTESS: Ladies and gentlemen, a pleasant surprise. A charming new acquain-

tance of mine. I hope that we shall welcome her joyously into our friendly
little circle. Maria . . . excuse me, I didn't quite catch your name?

STRANGER: Maria.

HOSTESS: But . . . the rest of your name?

STRANGER: Maria. My name is Maria.

HOSTESS: Very well, dear. I shall call you: Mary. There's something odd about
you, isn't there? But that only means we'll spend an even more enjoyable
evening with our delightful guest. Isn't that right, ladies and gentlemen?

(*They are all embarrassed. An awkward silence. The Host notices that one of the
guests has slipped off into the hall, and he goes out after him. The whispering of
someone excusing himself can be heard and the words: "not feeling entirely well." The
Poet remains motionless.*)

HOSTESS: So perhaps our marvelous poet will continue the reading at the point
where he was forced to break off. Mary dear, when you came in, our famous
poet was just reading to us . . . reading to us.

POET: Forgive me. Allow me to read some other time. I beg to be excused.

(*No one expresses any disappointment. The Poet goes over to the Hostess, who for a
while makes imploring gestures, but soon stops. The Poet sits quietly in a distant corner. He looks pensively at the Stranger. A maid passes around the sort of things usually
served on such occasions. A laugh, a few separate words, and occasionally whole
phrases emerge from the senseless babble of indistinct voices.*)

VOICES: No, how she danced! You just listen to me! The Russian intelligentsia
. . .

SOMEONE: (*In an exceptionally loud voice.*) You won't get it either! You won't get
it either!

(*Everyone has forgotten about the Poet. He gets up slowly from his place. He puts his
hand on his forehead. He takes a few steps back and forth across the room. From the
look on his face it is clear that he is making an agonizing effort to recall something. At
this point the words: "Rochefort" and "Camembert" become audible above the indistinct babble of voices. Then all of a sudden a fat man, in a state of frightful excitement, and making circular gestures, bounds into the middle of the room and shouts.*)

FAT MAN: Brie!

(*Suddenly the Poet stops his pacing. For a moment it seems that he has remembered
everything. He takes a few quick steps in the direction of the Stranger. But his path is
blocked by the Astrologer, who comes in from the hall wearing a civil servant's azure
uniform.*)

ASTROLOGER: Excuse me for being late and for wearing my civil servant's uniform. I came straight from a conference. I had to deliver a lecture. On astronomy . . . (*He points his finger upward.*)

HOST: (*Coming over.*) We were just talking about gastronomy. Ninochka, isn't it time we had supper?

HOSTESS: (*Getting up.*) Ladies and gentlemen, may I request your company? This way.

(*They all go out after her. The Stranger, the Astrologer, and the Poet remain for a while in the drawing room where it has grown darker and darker. The Poet and the Astrologer stand by the door, ready to leave. The Stranger lingers in the background by the dark half-opened curtains on the window.*)

ASTROLOGER: So we've chanced to meet again. I'm very glad. But let the circumstances of our first meeting remain strictly confidential.

POET: I ask the same of you.

ASTROLOGER: I have just given a lecture to the astronomical society—about the event to which you were an involuntary witness. A startling fact: a star of the first magnitude . . .

POET: Yes, it's very interesting.

ASTROLOGER: (*Rhapsodically.*) Yes, it certainly is! I entered in my records a new section: "A star called Maria has fallen!" For the first time science . . . Oh, forgive me for not asking you about the results of your search . . .

POET: My search has proved to be in vain.

(*He turns towards the back of the room. He looks about hopelessly. On his face apathy is discernible, and in his eyes emptiness and gloom. He reels under the frightful strain. But he has forgotten everything.*)

HOSTESS: (*On the threshold.*) Gentlemen! Come to the dining room! I don't see Mary . . . (*She threatens them with her finger.*) Oh, you young people! Have you hidden my Mary somewhere? (*She looks inquiringly at the back of the room.*) Where has Mary gone? Oh, where has Mary gone?

(*By the dark curtain there is no longer anyone at all. Through the window a bright star can be seen. Azure snow is falling, as azure as the civil servant's uniform worn by the Astrologer, who has disappeared.*)

END

The Jaws of Night

Fragment of a Planned Mystery

Andrei Bely

Written from 1898
Published 1907
Translated by Daniel Gerould

The corner of a plateau in the mountains, the last refuge of the Christians, cut off from the rest of the world by deep abysses. It is dark. The lace formed by the stars is pale and misty. To the right, the edge of a cypress grove. To the left, enormous rocks. The mountain plateau comes to an abrupt end in a steep precipice that plunges down to the depths. Along the edge of the precipice there is a stone railing. White patches glow in the depths of the night: these are glacial mountain peaks on the far side of the abyss. To the left, out of sight behind the rocks, stands an oil lamp whose flickering yellow gleams illumine this corner of the plateau. The yellow light falls in dull spots on the white costumes. The Christian women, tightly covered from head to foot, have gathered to pray before retiring for the long night. The prayer is now over, but they are loath to part without exchanging a few words. There are prophetesses among them. At least two or three are present. Their long gray hair falls down over their shoulders as a mark of sorrow and contrition. At the very brink, an old prophet, sunk in deep catatonic sleep, has leaned his white head against the railing. On his knees rests the delicate head of a frail little boy with hair white as flax. They are both asleep. The two of them, like marble statues, stand out vividly against the black night. Around the old man there is a semi-circle of greenish phosphorescent light that illumines the im- mediate vicinity. As they approach the railing, the Christian women become il- luminated by a slight glow and grow radiant. When they leave the lighted area, they continue for a while to radiate an almost tangible aureole, which then gradually goes out. The Christian women speak in a constrained and hushed tone of voice.

A CHRISTIAN WOMAN: Twenty-four hours have passed. And the day has not re- appeared.

A SECOND: There has been no day for a long time now. A cold night has taken its place. Only the moon has risen and set. The sun has not appeared.

A THIRD: But sisters, what if the sun never appears again? What if the sun at its last crimson setting has said farewell to us forever and forever: what if the sun has gone to its eternal rest?

ALL: The sun has disappeared . . .

A PROPHETESS: (*To the Third Christian Woman.*) Shame upon you, sister. Mortal anguish has hemmed us in. But we must burn away this anguish in the flame of hope. Are we not all doomed to death in any case?

THIRD: (*Endeavoring to smile.*) I do not complain, my mother. I knew the fate I was choosing.

AN OLD CHRISTIAN WOMAN: (*Seated on a rock.*) Since then three years have passed, three long years. We have suffered much.

PROPHETESS: (*Picking up a silver censer and blowing on the grains of incense.*) Let us suffer patiently a little longer, my children. Our sufferings will not last forever.

ALL: We keep the faith. We shall die in this faith.

THIRD: How sad it is not to see the sun. It was warm and golden. Now the sun has disappeared.

SECOND: And the day, how beautiful it was! Now golden, now bright as dew, now white as pearl. Dazzling splendor. Vistas open on all sides. And all of it crystal clear.

FIRST: Both the day and the light were God given. But we did not value his gifts. We did not offer up thanks to God. We did not compose prayers in honor of the golden day, nor hymns in honor of the rose-colored dawn. The Lord has taken away the dawn, and the Lord has taken away the day. And we bemoan our fate, like poor lost sheep.

SECOND: And yet not long ago it was different. You could sing on a sunny day, drenched in the bright beams. Sorrow might hang heavy upon your shoulders, but underfoot there were sunny spots and patches. You could sing in those beams. And now . . .

THIRD: Look here, what sort of place is this for song? Have we any reason to sing? Amongst us no song will ever be heard. (*Raising her eyes towards the black heavens.*) Unless perhaps up there? . . .

PROPHETESS: (*Lifting the censer to her trembling mouth, she blows upon it through parched lips. The grains of incense begin to smoulder. A ghostly little puff of flame trails off into smoke. The smoke rings, floating past the sleeping elder, acquire a bright glow of their own.*) There . . . There . . . What is the use of moans and groans? When there was light, we rejoiced. Now that the light is gone, we shall manage without it somehow. We shall endure everything. (*She stands erect and begins to go up and down the rows of Christian women swinging the censer. The women bow down, like white lilies swayed by a gentle breeze. She moves off behind the rocks. The faint clang of the censer continues to resound.*)

A CHRISTIAN WOMAN: Why do we gather together here every night for the burning of incense? It is so cold here. The wind beats against our breasts with an icy blast.

SECOND: Sister, don't you know that our prayer strengthens this mountain citadel? This is a place of danger. It is here that the attack will begin when the black hosts assail us. Our prayers hang in the night like an invisible force. Clouds of an invisible force surround our mountain fortress. Seen from below, we sem enveloped in storm clouds. The entire base of the mountain is shaken by the roar of thunder. But once our prayers weaken, the invisible force protecting us will melt away like a cloud, and the Lord will deliver us into the hands of the enemy. (*The Prophetess returns.*)

PROPHETESS: I have just looked down into the abysses. The clouds that girdled us like a shield of storm and smoke have been torn asunder. This is a sign that our prayers have weakened. Children, children, I do not reproach you for your weakness, for indeed a swiftly approaching end has been prophesied for us all. Like candles, we shall melt away in mortal anguish, and our enemies will triumph over us. But up there we shall shine brighter than the stars. (*She points to the black jaws of the heavens. The Christian women look upwards, but gloomy darkness invades their souls.*)

THIRD: How terrifying to blaze in so black a chasm when all the gulfs of creation lie beneath us.

PROPHETESS: But love will overcome all. The stars are flaming souls cast in the sky since time immemorial. (*Silence.*)

A CHRISTIAN WOMAN: (*Pointing to the sleeping Prophet.*) The holy elder sleeps a peaceful sleep. Look, a greenish light is spreading all around him. He is at the center of a luminous spot, and this luminous spot has lighted us as well. There is warmth and light when one draws near to him. Now he gives off a moon-like brilliance, but when he awakes, he will shine like the sun.

A SECOND CHRISTIAN WOMAN: It is only now that he has begun to glow. When God deprived the earth of day, the holy men became revealed. Now they are our only inextinguishable lanterns. Sometimes you make your way through the dark night, and suddenly in the distance you see a little green firefly. It is a holy man or holy woman moving through the darkness of the night. (*In a whisper.*) There is one amongst us who shines brighter than the sun, but he dwells in a cave and will come to us only in our hour of mortal danger. They say that the great Nikita . . .

A CHRISTIAN WOMAN: (*Placing her finger against her lips.*) Hush, of that we are not allowed to speak, not even in a whisper.

THIRD: (*Pointing to the sleeping boy, whose face, illuminated by a greenish glow, has become rigidly fixed in an expression of delirious rapture: he is dreaming indescribable dreams.*) Whose little boy is that?

SECOND: That is Anna's grandson. For whole days now he has not left the holy elder. (*Endeavoring to laugh.*) The old and the young . . .

THIRD: Where does the holy elder come from?

FIRST: I do not know. I remember having met him in the mountains. He joined us when we fled here. They say that he had come down from a pole: he used to be a stylite. It was in those days that he first appeared.

SECOND: Many others appeared then. And many have died for the faith. Few remain among us. (*Points with both hands to the elder.*) He is one of the few. The very few. He and the Great Nikita—they are our only guides.

PROPHETESS: But the hour when we must hide in caves and temples is close at hand. At such hours God's sentries are the only ones who stand guard the length of our fortress. We must not see what happens then in our absence. At such hours evil gales begin to blow. The north wind is harmful for us all.

THIRD: But how can we leave the holy elder alone in this dangerous place, alone with a defenseless child?

PROPHETESS: The child is pure. The enemy who lurks beyond the abyss cannot harm him. And the holy man does not fear the north wind. Let us go.

ALL: It is time! The air is growing icy. The wind is rising. It is time.

(*They move off into the cypress grove. The mysterious Prophet, congealed in a rigid pose, seems a marble statue. The glow of his halo is radiant. The child opens his deep blue eyes in astonishment. He is small and frail, and his nervous laugh is like the ringing of a tiny bell. He shouts in the ear of the rigidly immobile elder.*)

CHILD: Grandfather! Grandfather! Grandfather!

PROPHET: (*Without regaining consciousness.*) Eh? What? has it already begun?

CHILD: (*With a melancholy, silvery laugh.*) Nothing has begun. Always the same darkness.

PROPHET: (*Falling asleep again.*) Uh . . .

CHILD: (*Tugging at the elder.*) But wake up.

PROPHET: (*Rubbing his eyes.*) Nothing has begun. Always the same darkness. (*He turns to the child suddenly with the caressing tenderness of a very old man.*) What is the matter, little one?

CHILD: Oh, grandfather, you are so strange. At one moment you are totally deaf, and at the next you see and hear better than all of us.

PROPHET: (*Passes his dazzling palm over the child's white hair, causing lilac-colored electric sparks to shoot forth.*) When the Lord gives me his support, then I see and hear and speak. But there are times when I neither hear, nor see (*he smiles, and it seems as if a sudden bolt of lightning had licked the mass of rocks*), nor speak. (*His face gradually grows illuminated, and the pale moon-like glow of his nimbus changes into a white light like that of the sun. The bright glow spreads slowly, making his face appear severe and strange.*)

CHILD: (*Caressing the old man.*) My dear, dear white grandfather. You are old. Why are you covered with bright netting? I shall grab hold of one of those bright-colored threads and wind it into a luminous little ball. And I shall bring it to mama. Mama is always careful to hide such little balls: that, she says, is holiness.

PROPHET: (*Threatening him playfully with his finger.*) Not so fast, you naughty boy. The same fate is reserved for all. For the old and for the young. (*He spreads his hands apart in a resigned gesture.*) In times like these, do not expect too much. Oh, my clever little bee: would you really gather holiness from me, as though it were honey, even though I am a great sinner? Not so fast.

Not in times like these.

CHILD: And what sort of times are these, grandfather? That is what mother always says too: *in times like these.* Have there ever been other times not like these times? What other times are there?

PROPHET: (*Laughing.*) There are many kinds of other times.

CHILD: (*Insistently.*) But what kinds of other times?

PROPHET: Well, for example, day time. We do not have day time any longer. Now there is no more day. And night time, my dear boy, is dark.

CHILD: But I remember the day.

PROPHET: You are still too small, my child, to know what terror is; but you must realize that the day is a blessing from God, and that we have been deprived of this paradise: there is no more day.

CHILD: (*Smiling nervously, while at the same time his eyes remain grave and wide open.*) But we can live like this and get along without the day. I shall break off this piece of netting from your clothes and bring it to mama. She will light the cave with it. And that will be our day. (*He grabs the Prophet playfully by his clothes and runs off to one side. In his closed fist there remains a luminous trace, but it melts away like a tiny little cloud.*) You see?

PROPHET: Child, child . . . (*He sighs deeply. He bows his one-hundred-year-old head pensively. Silence.*)

CHILD: Grandfather, when did times like these times of ours begin?

PROPHET: (*Almost harshly.*) When they built the Temple of Glory. When it was defiled by an evil king. Surely your mother told you about that, didn't she?

CHILD: (*Gaily.*) Why, yes, of course she told me. But just where is this Temple of Glory?

PROPHET: (*His brightness grown dim and his nimbus almost gone.*) Only the ruins remain. The green waves of the sea wash the ruins. And the Temple of Glory has ceased to exist.

CHILD: (*In a subdued tone of voice.*) And then what happened?

PROPHET: (*Harshly, after a moment's silence.*) Then there was an evil king.

CHILD: (*Having kept quiet for a while.*) And now?

PROPHET: (*Reluctantly.*) And now there is an evil king too.

CHILD: (*Glancing fearfully at the Prophet who has grown dimmer and dimmer.*) And where does he reign?

PROPHET: (*Thrusting his dried-up right hand lifelessly into the gloomy darkness beyond the abyss.*) He is there . . . In the north.

(*Deep silence. Having lost his brightness, the Prophet sits leaning on his bony elbow. The little boy touches him in terror; a dry crackling can be heard, and a stinging lightning bolt strikes his tiny finger. The wind blows; the cypresses whisper like murderers awaiting execution. From the distant heights comes the scarcely audible cry of the nightwatchman: "He that hath ears to hear, let him hear."*)

PROPHET: (*Whispers to himself.*) He that leadeth into captivity shall go into captivity. He that killeth with the sword must be killed with the sword.

CHILD: (*Grabbing hold of the Prophet's clothing.*) It is cold. Take me away from here.

PROPHET: (*Having lost his radiance, he leans his elbows on the railing. Covering his eyes with his hand, he breathes in the darkness.*) A wind from beyond the clouds. A wind which blows from the other side of the mountains. More news. Bad news from the north.

CHILD: (*Grabbing hold of the Prophet's clothing.*) It is cold. Take me away from here.

(*From the far-off peaks comes the faintly audible voice: "He that hath ears to hear, let him hear."*)

PROPHET: (*After a moment's silence, as though to himself, he answers the cry.*) He that leadeth into captivity shall go into captivity. He that killeth with the sword must be killed with the sword.

CHILD: (*Almost in tears.*) Grandfather, what are you muttering to yourself?

PROPHET: (*Regaining his self-possession, in a different and gentler tone of voice.*) My child, I am saying my prayers. (*For an instant his face becomes illuminated by a bright glow and then grows dark again immediately thereafter.*)

CHILD: It is cold. Take me away from here.

PROPHET: (*Having lost his radiance, he leans his elbows on the railing. Covering his eyes with his hand, he breathes in the darkness.*) A wind from beyond the clouds. A wind which blows from the other side of the mountains. More news. Bad news from the north.

CHILD: The wind, but why is it like this . . .

PROPHET: (*Interrupting him, as though fearing that what should not be said might be said.*) Because it comes from an evil kingdom . . .

CHILD: So an evil king lives beyond the mountains?

PROPHET: (*Thrusting his dried-up right hand lifelessly into the gloomy darkness beyond the abyss.*) Over there . . . Over there . . . Through the clouds . . through the creeping fog . . . (*The cry of the sentry is heard closer at hand and more urgently.*)

CHILD: What does he cry out so often for? When I fall asleep at home in my own little bed and hear that cry, I feel like weeping.

PROPHET: (*Trying to calm him.*) That is the nightwatchman. He is for us. During the night he makes the rounds of the citadel. He peers into the darkness. He does not want anything bad to happen to us under cover of night.

CHILD: Why does he cry out so often?

PROPHET: He is warning us to be on our guard.

CHILD: Is it really so dangerous here?

PROPHET: (*Gravely.*) Yes, perhaps it is. (*Silence. The Prophet suddenly straightens up his bent frame. His powerful build now becomes striking. Bright beams fly off his body and shafts of light stream forth from his illumined head. A luminous spot spreads across his stooped back. His hair, as though saturated with electricity, stands up all over his head. He jumps up on the railing. Standing erect above the chasm, he cries out in a resounding voice, cupping his hand around his mouth.)* I see and hear.

CHILD: *(Grabbing hold of the Prophet's iridescent clothing, he gives a tug and comes running into the circle of light beams, but in his hands there only remain radiant tatters that take on the shape of sweet-smelling flower cups.)* Grandfather, you will fall into the abyss! Good heavens, what a sweet smell . . . These are not scraps of cloth that I hold in my hands, they are little flowers, they are little flowers . . . And now a golden bee alights on a bright little flower as it sways in the beams of the sun. It is no solitary bee, but, look, whole swarms of velvety little bees are dancing luminously around you. And you stay there, with your hands outstretched over the precipice . . . Grandfather, grandfather, my head is spinning.

PROPHET: *(Turning his face, but it is impossible to make out the features, because his head is ablaze with dazzling brilliance.)* I am not afraid of the abysses: the hour of God's will has come. The powers of darkness are marching against us.

(In the distance the cry of the sentry can be heard in answer to the prophetic call of the old man: "What do you see and what do you hear, you who keep the watch?")

PROPHET: *(Blossoming with blue, red, and green beams of light, he cries out.)* I see the mists, I hear the wailing of the wind in the mountains.

(Answer of the sentry: "These are ill-omened signs.")

CHILD: *(He runs towards the rocks, trailing behind him a luminous veil of thin haze. He cries out in ecstasy.)* From you I have plucked a violet that will never fade. You are all covered with violets; God's bees, God's golden bees, are flying after me! Mama, I shall bring you a little bouquet, I shall come to you all bright and shining. I am bearing holiness in my hands, I am bearing holiness like a tiny handful of brightness. *(He runs off.)*

(The darkness becomes illuminated. Luminous spots appear here and there in the depths of the gloom, lighting up the distant contours of the mountain plateau. If one looks attentively, it is possible to make out a venerable old man in the center of each of the spots: all these venerable old men have come to the edge of the precipice in order to answer the enemy challenge in a worthy manner. They shine like fire-flies or precious stones. Along the edges of the plateau it seems that a joyous illumination has been lighted.)

VOICE TO THE RIGHT: Arise, people of God!

VOICE TO THE LEFT: Arm yourself with the sword of prayer!

VOICE TO THE RIGHT: Black clouds are marching against you.

VOICE TO THE LEFT: What a strange cloud.

VOICE TO THE RIGHT: Look down into the precipice. What a night . . .

VOICE TO THE LEFT: Oh, oh, oh. I have looked down. I have seen a black cloud creeping towards us. Clouds like that have not appeared since the flood. What will it pour down upon us?

VOICE TO THE RIGHT: That cloud has been hurled down at us from under the protective circle of storm clouds which were rent asunder today because our prayers grew faint-hearted. It has been hurled into the breach.

VOICE TO THE LEFT: Oh, oh, oh.

VOICE TO THE RIGHT: The cloud is passing by. It was an innocent cloud, flying low beneath the shield of clouds. Because of the prayers of the just the shield of clouds has closed again. Once more the mountain fortress trembles with an invisible force.

(*In the distance one hears the voice of the nightwatchman: "Be calm and do not awaken the people: it was a false alarm." The little green lights containing holy men gradually go out. The illuminated edges of the plateau are once again plunged into darkness. Once again it seems that there is nothing there, absolutely nothing.*)

PROPHET: (*Coming down from the railing.*) There is still time. Our forces are not yet exhausted. Oh, Lord, do not forsake us! (*He goes towards the rocks. His face is uplifted to the heavens. His blue eyes seem huge sapphires. His clothing, covered with beams of light, undulates behind him. A luminous circle floats around him. Colored lights of various hues dance along the edges of this luminous circle. It is like flowers opening or beetles—golden, pearly, bright, beautiful—dancing.*)

MOTHER'S VOICE: My child, where are you? The night is long and sad. Answer, my child, answer from the depths of the black night. (*She appears, dressed in long black robes.*)

PROPHET: He was with me. He has run off to your cave. Why do you come out at such a late hour? Now only innocent children and old men walk about in the gloom of the night. You must wait until the morning hours. If you meet the nightwatchman, he will punish you.

MOTHER: Let him. But the morning hours will bring me no consolation. The hours of morning are black hours. Now all the hours are black. Black jaws will swallow us all. Old men, what have you done to these innocent children by luring us here to this black isle?

PROPHET: (*Pointing with his luminous finger to the black jaws of the heavens.*) But up there we shall shine brighter than the stars.

MOTHER: (*Grasping her head in her hands.*) I do not wish to blaze in so black a chasm. Old man, old man, save your words for others. (*Pointing to his aureole*.) Take off that peacock's tail of yours: it will not persuade me of anything. Answer me, answer me, why have you Christians carried us off to this gloomy lair, when He, joyous and free, has transformed life into a light-hearted melody?

PROPHET: (*Angrily*.) But God has deprived us of the day.

MOTHER: (*Filled with the spirit*.) That is not true! To see the sun it suffices to go a few hundred leagues from here. It is all your fault, old men with your magic spells. (*In tears*.) I do not weep for myself, but for our children. Why are these innocent angels doomed to death and destruction? They are innocent angels, innocent angels . . . For a long time I idolized you, old man, I kept my lair bright and tidy by the magic lights with which you shine. I rejoiced to see an old man and an innocent angel become such loving friends. But you have poisoned the soul of even that angel. The angel has grown fatally enamored of night and death.

(*The Prophet, threatening her angrily with his finger, withdraws among the rocks. Taciturn and menacing, he disappears. The light vanishes with him. Everything is plunged into black night. The Mother, like a despairing ghost, passes silently beneath the grove of cypresses. The Child enters. Something golden glitters in his hands, and they give off a feeble radiance.*)

CHILD: Grandfather, dear, white grandfather! One by one I have dropped handfuls of holiness; now holiness blooms barrenly at night in luminous pale-blue violets. Grandfather, give me holiness.

MOTHER: (*Rushing over to the child, she kisses his hands and feet with stifled sobs.*) Why, oh, why? These angelic little hands, these precious little feet condemned to be crucified? Out of sheer madness the night-time murderer has resolved to poison the innocent breath of life. We had faith, we abandoned ourselves to these mad fancies, and now our angels, our poor little angels, must perish.

CHILD: Mama, mama, golden bees gather about the old man, flying and buzzing. Mama, do not weep, I shall make you a present of grace. (*He throws her a handful of brightness, and the mother's black garments become covered with golden spots, and luminous little flowers blossom on the ground.*) Do you see those little ruby crosses? They sway back and forth on one tiny little stem; it is a carnation. And here there are little white crosses: it is a violet. Not a carnation, not a violet, but holiness . . . (*He plucks the little flowers.*) What perfume, what sweetness. Mama, what are you crying for then? (*Sadly*.) I feel like crying too. (*He examines the flowers which melt away slowly in his hands. Swirling like a scarcely perceptible little cloud, holiness melts away in the chasm of the night.*) The little flowers are going out. They are going out. (*Silence*.) Mama. (*He nestles up against the sobbing woman. He weeps.*) It is frightful. I am afraid. I am afraid.

(*Total darkness. The voice of the nightwatchman is heard from the heights: "Who is wandering in the mountains and in the valleys at this forbidden hour?"*)

VOICE: (*Drawing near.*) Who are you? Answer . . .

(*From out of the blackness in which both mother and child are engulfed there is heard only a deep, sorrowful voice full of despair: "Woe!" A strong wind blows and the clump of cypresses, no longer illumined by a bright glow, moans like a host of souls in torment.*)

END

The Ballad of the Seven
Sleeping Brothers in China

Tadeusz Miciński

Written sometime between 1905 and 1910
Published 1934
First performance: Theatre STU, Łódź, 1969
Translated by Daniel Gerould and Jadwiga Kosicka

An insane asylum surrounded by a large forest. A rectangular ward where the madmen either stand or lie—the Doctor in a white apron leads in the Poet. The Poet carries a branch of flowering plane-tree and a small traveling bag.

MADMEN: (*All around.*) That scoundrel is jeering at us. Instead of an electric eel, he has fished up for us out of the sea a poisonous scorpion.

(*In the distance, a doleful tune on a reed pipe can be heard.*)

DOCTOR: My good sir, this will be your place of residence until you can rid yourself of the notion that you are married to someone else's wife. You have been laboring under this delusion for three years now. Aren't you growing tired of it?

POET: Do you know Bronzino's painting "Youth"—the one with the medieval city in the background?

DOCTOR: Perhaps I do. But I don't have time to waste on things like that. What are you trying to get at?

POET: What I am trying to get at doesn't matter in the least; it is your affair what conclusions you draw. That woman, as you have called her, became mine the moment she first fixed her gaze on me—her eyes say more than all those volumes of literature so esteemed by you and your kind. It is in this fashion that all the madonnas in the world have been created. I call her Domina Aurea because gold is the synthesis of all colors and in medieval mysticism it symbolizes perfect happiness, or in other words, heaven.

DOCTOR: Why have you gone so pale?

POET: I saw before me a vast rocky desert on which nothing grew and the only thing standing was a single-storied house in the Hindu style, and there behind half-open shutters I saw her: she was sitting on the floor crying, her hair loose and flowing.

DOCTOR: You will take a sedative and I'll give you a powerful astringent.

POET: It is your task only to recommend the treatment; it is for me to judge it worthy of commemoration in the mirror which Erasmus of Rotterdam has written.

DOCTOR: (*Frowning.*) And just what is that, if I may ask?

POET: A mirror of imponderable things, that is to say, those which cannot be pondered.

DOCTOR: (*Calling an attendant with a sign of his hand.*) Put him in a uniform; he seems clean, he doesn't need a bath; see that my prescription is filled; for the evening meal, half the usual portion. (*To the Poet.*) I'll say good-bye for now, try to make the best of your stay here. You are not the only poet to whom this has happened: there was also Torquato Tasso, Swift, Gogol, and, it seems, even Słowacki, according to what the academic authorities say.

(*The Poet stands with his eyes fixed on the rays of the setting sun. He remains silent. The Doctor goes out.*)

MADMEN: You see—he really is a poet! How do you do, Mr. Shake-Spear.

ANOTHER: Perhaps he is Aladdin with his lamp taken away.

ANOTHER: He looks like God ashamed of his abortive work.

ANOTHER: He is the destroyer, I recognized him by his stealthy step when he stole in among us to blot the sun from our sight. To further the cause of justice I shall have him hanged in the belfry among the bells. From that belfry they will toll only for the dead.

POET: (*Rousing himself.*) If you wouldn't mind taking your places, gentlemen— any of these seats here near me—I shall try to offer you a performance in this amphitheatre of ours.

OLD MAN: (*With the face of Hoene-Wroński.*) We accept your proposal. I, Sardanapalus the mathematician, could be the drunken gravedigger.

ANOTHER: And I shall be joyful Job when he took a new wife and then had to beget a new flock.

ANOTHER: Sapristi! We'll start a Cabaret des Noctambules. Like a prostitute I'll entertain you all today, only just buy me an absinthe.

OTHERS: (*Clapping their hands and dancing.*) Let's begin the performance.

OTHERS: (*Standing gloomily in corners.*) Just keep away from us—for we have been condemned and whoever takes one step further will fall into an abyss where the frightful worm gnaws and bites with eternal flames.

ANOTHER: And here I am, Rosa Luxemburg, and through me lies the way to the Hen-House where the hens roost and lay eggs of universal contentment. Your Excellency, light my lantern. I consider it proper to squeeze out the brains of everyone with this taxation screw.

ANOTHER: But what does it matter if only their souls are on the road to Calvary.

ANOTHER: Now we are going to the House of Parliament where they have just declared war on the absurd. You can be sure there won't be any place left for what's called life.

ANOTHER: Who will light my holy candle for me, I should like to play cards
since God has just begun shuffling the cards.

ANOTHER: Listen, the drunken gravedigger is starting to sing.

OLD MAN:

The virgins all approach my hand
each brings a crown of roses. Like grooms
they lead my horse and on command
they go into the dust of tombs.
Mistresses whose pelvis swells
Cake-Walk dancing all around
don't you hear the pealing bells?
Naked Satan comes in a bound!
Women with your sacred thighs
teach me all your several faiths.
Dead in my coffin, I arise
O'er tomb-like caverns—King of Wraiths!

POET: Oh, gravedigger, you have made a fine start, yea, verily, Satan is present here, and in the event this fact is more important than God himself. Let
us start the performance.

FIRST GUARD: Listen, this is no merry-go-round, you have to behave yourself
and eat your half-portion.

ANOTHER: We beseech you, good brother, don't make us stop—for in a moment darkness will come whatever we do.

OLD MAN: Can't you comprehend that no one exists, there is no you—only
my soul exists and the sun. The sun is crucified on billions of numerals, but
now it will be resurrected so that it can give itself to me. The sun is the eternal woman. Oh, solar Medusa, do you love me?

POET: She said: no!

OLD MAN: I have nothing more to say to anyone.

OTHERS: This performance gets a half-portion too, Mr. Shake-Spear. The sun
has lighted your holy candle for you, come along—since you're supposed to
play cards with God.

SCHOLAR: I propose that none of us get carried away by the whirling torrents
of fantasy; let us examine reality in cold blood. We are a small band of people whose ideas have lost all validity. This man is *homo religans* out of the
Middle Ages. He has a feeling, acquired amongst mankind, for cathedrals
and the mass; some of you are relics from the paleocene epoch and you
would be more at home in a cave sucking out the marrow of a deer than
being born Poles at the beginning of the twentieth century.

POET: (*Slowly, solemnly.*) Listen, all of you, I'll tell you about my strange experience which I shall call *The Ballad of the Seven Sleeping Brothers In China.*
(*They all quiet down. Some attempt to catch flies which are whirling in the rays of*

the setting sun.) On a rocky desert where nothing grows, there stands a house in the Hindu style. I entered after flinging wide the door and passed through many a strange chamber adorned with frescoes which depicted landscapes from other planets, such as a sapphire lake and by it various rocks and flowers which do not exist here. Proceeding further, I noticed a chamber where seven knights slept on seven beds and in the middle of the room on an altar with a huge mirror and seven burning lamps lay a Chinese Princess whose great black eyes were opened wide and fixed upon a knight who was scarcely more than a lad. She did not move when I entered, but I noticed that a small mirror which she held on the altar suddenly became enveloped in a mist shaped like a chrysanthemum. And she spoke to me very softly so that the sleepers would not hear. "Throw the youngest of these sleepers into a deep cistern after you have first removed his garments, and wear them yourself. Once you have performed this sacrifice, lie down on the bed and try not to fall asleep." I went over to the sleeping knight and seeing that the lad was sound asleep, I began to unbuckle his armor; it was all I could do to take his sword out of his hand, then holding him naked as he threw his arms around my neck, I carried him to the edge of the cistern and set him down, not daring to throw him in. I returned to the chamber wearing his armor and lay down on the bed with his sword and tried not to fall asleep. Thereupon the silence grew so immense that nothing could be heard but the pounding of our blood-drenched hearts—for I could hear the blood drip ever so softly from our hearts as though from brim-full goblets, and creating strange, mutually repellent designs on the parquet floor. Something in the shape of luxuriant flora climbed the walls and filled the chamber; soon it bore crystal flowers and fruits resembling those which snow and frost create on icy trees in the Cave of Ice. (*The guards try to break up the meeting. Screams.*) Dazzling brightness overcame me and I was like a flower in a hot-house, saturated by the deadly, poisonous rays of the sun. Splendid music seized possession of me, as the domes of vast temples rose up and whirled by ceaselessly in the immense silence. I, last but one of the Christs, had nought to do but fix my gaze on the figure of the Chinese Princess as wise as though her forehead had been cast by Tao himself in his moment of greatest inspiration. The seeds were peering out from within the ripened fruits—these were truths not yet apt for that rocky desert. (*Silence again.*) Aromas from strange, uncanny flowers spread throughout the air—and you, sleeping knights, and I, sole nay-sayer to the dream, imbibed that fragrance stranger than the Nostalgia for a different life from which we suffer, we who are born and not yet totally mocked by the Earth. Suddenly the Princess rose up and, carrying the small mirror, went over to the oldest of the sleepers who now had a graying beard and the garb of a Black Magus—dotted with numerals—she held the mirror up—and I saw to my utmost horror that he was crumbling into a heap of bones and dust.

OLD MAN: You've figured out who I am, you imp!

POET: Thereupon the Princess went over to another Knight and did the same to him—with this difference only that of this wayfaring Sailor nothing was left but a cloud congealing into ice. And thus it was with the others—I no longer recall, but one of them sizzled on contact with the mirror like an iron when water splashes against it—and a deep cavern formed in his face—and a huge crater in the parquet floor in which his weariness took refuge. At last the Princess came over to me and held the mirror above me and I felt wings grow out of me so gigantic that they tore down the walls and roof and bore all of you on their feathers like light hoar-frost—you whose name is mankind.

MADMEN: But we weren't there!

POET: You were the atmosphere of that house—and I was the only one left, my wings growing, and then the Chinese Princess showed me the cistern in the other room. Having drawn poisoned water from the cistern, I created Everlasting Stillness out of this water, and there was silence amongst the thickets. The Princess and I went out onto the terrace. We were alone. The last and youngest of the semblances of reality lay quietly on the brink. We were alone, the two of us on the terrace, amidst the infinite rocky desert. The sun had just set.

MADMEN: You have bored us, and we bribed the guards in vain to have the show prolonged. Now we're breaking up—everyone's supper has grown cold —let's all go to bed—to sleep, to dream and thereby ward off the painful thought that we exist.

OLD MAN: (*Solemnly, but with a smile.*) I bid you farewell; we are the Sleeping Knights—woe to you whose eyes are open and who endeavor not to sleep.

(*Heavy dusk has now fallen, there can be heard only smacking sounds and the groans and sighs of those praying. The guards bring in two night lamps.*)

POET: (*In sudden terror.*) Let me out! Let me out! Don't lock me in here for the night—I am not a madman, I swear it to my Spirit Pure as the Statue of Magical Immovable Energy. Let me out—or else lunacy will get me into its clutches. Let me out—I've been buried here in this grave of madness for three years already—I feel my armor starting to crack—and a claw cuts me to the heart. (*Wrestling with the guards.*) Let me out—I am not Christ that I should die in agony on this Golgotha.

GUARDS: The strait jacket! (*They put him in a strait jacket.*)

POET: Father, why hast Thou forsaken us?!

GUARDS: We've got to put him to bed—not so hard, we've wrenched his arm, there'll be trouble again like yesterday—it happens all the time with these poor wretches. One of them tries to get loose and seems strong, and all of a sudden he snaps in your hand.

SECOND GUARD: No more singing now.

OLD MAN: (*Singing.*)
 I'll spread pale shrouds and other graveyard things
 Come, virgins, to the antic dance with you
 My harp has seven colors as its strings
GUARD: Quiet now, quiet. No more of that—time for prayers.

(*Behind them a chorus of pious murmurs can be heard.*)

MADMEN:
 Good night, Sweet Jesus' Saintly head,
 That was run through the brain till dead
 Good night my rose in bloom
 Good night beloved groom
 Good night

(*The Guards go out, the Orderlies sit down in their easy chairs. A sullen quiet prevails, in which there can be heard only tossing and turning from the beds, and occasionally a nonsensical word, all by itself, cut off from everything else. All of a sudden the Poet's voice, soft as harp strings, resounds. He recites what is evidently poetry, but always in a completely different tone of voice than the words themselves demand: he expresses sad feelings joyously, and he portrays cheerful scenes with immense sadness. While the Poet declaims, only the Old Man sits up in his bed and listens with rapt attention.*)

POET: Chivalric sonnets
 I) There is a shining Unicorn who ever dips his only horn
  into the sea of pain—it grows at once as red as any rose—
  and like the fiery myth of flame
  to ashes burns the soul—oh, shame!

  It follows you, aloof, with footsteps faint,
  at times it laughs—but not without constraint,
  then lost in thought it waits, before the palace gates,
  where you see yourself gored with your very own sword.

  This Unicorn escorts you 'mongst a fellowship,
  Monsalvat's knights and ladies fair beyond belief,
  and you—hair-shirted, locked in silence's silent grip,
  which says: "Oh, Host of Hosts—deny not friends your grief!"

  The Cardinal shows you wind-swept walls, monastic, sad,
  grim fortress—sighs the wind: "Torquato Tasso's mad."
  From shame sinks down in darkest shades the fiery Unicorn.
  Oh, who will understand: at night vast gaze his eyes forlorn.

II) Through twilight gold I go towards Thee, oh, Mary
Monsalvat's slopes I climb subdued and tame.
Above me angels beat their golden wings.
The pulpit-man burns off my wounds with flame.

But disbelief, sad as a requiem, still sounds
its organ-notes—despair my bleeding hearts' refrain—
The mournful candles bloom 'midst Polish burial mounds—
the horse I ride, knight woeful, black with purple train.

From black abysses to Monsalvat I voyage afar
with sudden joy that spite of all I am redeemed!
Love ever sings in choir; now Lady more than star
comes toward me sibylline where once hell-doomed I seemed.

I climb high flights of stairs, the castle's sky-deep grave
And through me joy plays—golden Organs in the nave . . .

MADMEN: (*Waking up.*) You've no right to disturb sleeping Christians—put his
strait jacket on him—he'll strangle us—he took his strait jacket off!—he'll
strangle us—!

OLD MAN: What an old ass I've been to deceive myself for so many years with
such optimism, for so many years—(*He throws the Gospel out the window, outside the night wind can be heard moaning. The Poet moves about stealthily and
turns down the lamps.*)

POET: Do not think of me any more, try not to awaken—I am strolling with the
Princess along the terrace in the midst of the Infinite Desert.

(*The Guards spring up, light matches, and see that the Poet has pulled one arm out of
his strait jacket and hanged himself by his suspenders. The Madmen hide their heads
under the bedclothes and peer out furtively. One of the Guards runs off to call the
Doctor. The Doctor comes in.*)

DOCTOR: He was incurable, absolutely incurable. His brother is an even worse
imbecile, he should be locked up too. Take the body out. What's the point
of examining it? . . . It doesn't make any difference! . . .

(*They carry the dead body out. The Doctor leaves. The Guards once again take up
their places in their easy chairs. The quiet is interrupted only by the hissing of the
lamps. All of a sudden the lamps go out again. All the Madmen pull their bedclothes
over their heads. One of the Guards gets up and goes over to the window. The vast
glow of a dying Meteor is seen against the sky.*)

END

The Wayfarer

A Psychodrama in One Act

Valerii Briusov

CHARACTERS:

Julia, the daughter of a forester
Wayfarer, a non-speaking character

Written 1910
Published 1911
First performances: St. Petersburg and the provinces, 1911
                    Theatre-Casino, Terioki, Finland, July 6, 1913,
                    by Georges Pitoëff's "Our Theatre"
Translated by Daniel Gerould

A room in the forester's house. A wet, stormy night. The windows are closed and shuttered. The howling of the wind and the beating of the rain can be heard. The room is dimly lighted by a kerosene lamp. The stove is burning. Knocking at the gate. A dog barking.

JULIA: (*At the window, trying to peer through a gap in the shutter.*)
  Who's there?
  I cannot let you in: I am alone.
  Go to the miller's, along the path, to the left,
  Across the brook . . . But, look, you've got to stop
  That knocking now. You'll simply hurt your hands!
  The door is strong, you'll never break it in.
  There's not a chance I'll open up. And we've got
  A vicious dog. Be on your way in peace.
  The miller's place is less than two miles off.
  They'll let you in . . .
  (*Aside.*)   But he can really bang!

(*She moves away from the window. The knocking continues. The dog barks.*)

JULIA: (*She comes back to the window, but still does not open the shutters.*)
  Listen! Whatever your name is? You hear me talking:
  I am a young girl, and alone in the house,
  I do not know you. Then judge for yourself
  Whether I can let you in. What would
  The neighbors have to say about me if
  You spent the night with me! Out of the question!
  And, when he left, my father ordered me
  Not to let any one in. And what's so bad
  About your walking two miles under the pines?
  Well, rain is rain! You really won't get soaked.

(*Silence. Knocking at the gate. The dog barks.*)

JULIA: (*To herself.*)
    He just stands there and knocks . . . He looks so tired,
    And perhaps he's even sick. Since wedging himself
    Against the door-frame, he hasn't moved away,
    And, like a robot, beats the board with his hand.
    Just look, the poor boy's drenched right through. He's dressed
    In city clothes—he's young and pale—or so
    It seems to me, in the dark. He mustn't be
    From here, he doesn't know his way through the woods . . .
    Well, should I let him in?
    (*Aloud.*)   Listen! Tell me,
    Where are you from? Where are you going? Just what
    Do you want here? Do answer me! How can
    I let a total stranger in the house!
    What's wrong with you? Has the cat got your tongue?
    If you're planning to keep silent, then—
    Adieu, you've seen the last of me! Stay there.
    Keep on knocking till sunrise! Nothing on earth
    Will make me open.
(*She moves away from the window.*)
              Thinks he's someone grand!
    Some prince or other! Doesn't want to talk,
    Well, then, get drenched.
(*Silence. Knocking at the gate.*)
             Good heavens! He won't give
    Me any peace all night long. Or he'll die
    On my doorstep—that would be the last straw!
    A city boy in fancy clothes, got lost
    While walking, spied the house—and now won't leave.
    Afraid of wolves in the forest. The cursed nuisance!
    What can you do with him?
(*She goes to the window once again.*)
            Look here—what's wrong with you?
    Passer-by prince! Be so kind as to show
    That you don't have a weapon with you. Open
    Your overcoat! Now raise your hands, that's right . . .
    Well, fine! I'm sorry for you. I'm opening up.

(*She runs out. Sound of a bolt being slid back. A dog barking. Enter Julia and the Wayfarer, thoroughly drenched.*)

JULIA:
>The dog is on the chain, don't be afraid.
>Well, didn't you get soaked! Right through! Take off
>Your coat and boots. There's a lap robe on the bench—
>Take it, use it. Slippers are under the bench—
>Yes, put them on. That's good. Now just sit down,
>And warm yourself, I'll throw some wood in the stove.

WAYFARER: (*He takes off his overcoat and boots, puts on the slippers, and wraps himself up in the lap robe. Julia tosses logs into the stove.*)

JULIA: Want a little vodka? Well, go ahead!

(*She brings out the bottle and pours him a small glassful.*)

WAYFARER: (*He nods his head as a sign of appreciation and drinks.*)

JULIA: But there's nothing to eat, not even any bread.

WAYFARER: (*He shakes his head negatively, indicating that he is not hungry.*)

JULIA:
>Well, listen to me. For the night I'll give
>You this room here. The sofa's comfortable,
>Lie down, and sleep until tomorrow morning.
>And I will go to bed behind that partition.
>I've got a gun there, and if you come near
>The doorway, I shall instantly and with
>Unerring aim put a bullet through your head.
>And Polka will not let me be abused!
>You understand? Well then, we're friends for now.

WAYFARER: (*He nods his head.*)

JULIA: But why don't you say anything? Answer me!

WAYFARER: (*He makes a sign with his hand.*)

JULIA: What does that mean?

WAYFARER: (*He makes the same sign again.*)

JULIA:
>   I do not understand.
>   Or are you mute?

WAYFARER: (*He makes a sign that is neither affirmative nor negative.*)

JULIA:
>   I don't believe it. That's
>   Your way of trying to make fun of me!
>   Hey, watch out! I won't let you abuse me!

WAYFARER: (*He grabs Julia's hand and kisses it respectfully.*)

JULIA:
>   Well, that's enough, I didn't do a thing.
>   So then you're mute? Now it's all clear to me.

That's why you kept so silent all the while.
But you're not deaf?
WAYFARER: (*He shakes his head negatively.*)
JULIA: You understand me, don't you?
WAYFARER: (*He nods his head affirmatively.*)
JULIA:
Oh, oh, poor boy, poor boy! Come now, forgive me.
You see: my father left for town this morning,
Tomorrow he'll come back. The miller's two
Miles off, the village beyond the river, and no one
In the whole house. Just me and Polka. It's obvious
Why I was afraid to let a man in.
But you're completely different, dear. Why, you're
So pale and thin, and weak and sickly-looking.
You must be quite unhappy.
WAYFARER: (*He nods affirmatively.*)
JULIA:
But then, tell me:
Are you really from town? Do you live there?
WAYFARER: (*He shakes his head negatively.*)
JULIA: Not in the town? Then where? Far, far away?
WAYFARER: (*He nods his head affirmatively.*)
JULIA:
And what's your name? Sergei? Ivan? or Peter?
Nikita? Nikolai? or Alexander?
WAYFARER: (*He shakes his head negatively.*)
JULIA:
Well, what does it matter! I am Julia.
I'll call you Robert. That's a name that I
Have always liked a lot. So tell me, Robert,
Where were you going? To the mill? Or further,
To Otradnoye village? Or to the estate,
To the Voznitsins? Or even further still?
WAYFARER: (*He shakes his head negatively and covers his face with his hands.*)
JULIA: Don't want to tell me? What is it—a secret?
WAYFARER: (*He nods his head affirmatively.*)
JULIA:
A secret? Oh, that's what! Like in a novel?
I've read quite a few. Two years ago
There was a lady living in Otradnoye
Who used to give me books. I still have two
Of them now: *The Scullery-Maid Who Became Countess*
And *The Black Prince*. Have you read them?
WAYFARER: (*He shakes his head negatively.*)

JULIA:
                    Too bad.
I've read them eight times each at least, and still
Whenever I come to the touching scenes,
Right off I start to cry—I can't help it!
A Gypsy stole the Countess's baby daughter,
She didn't know she was herself a countess,
Grew up like a poor beggar, had to work,
And suddenly . . .
But then, I won't describe it all . . . Sometimes
The idea suddenly strikes me: what if
Instead of being a forester's daughter,
I too am a countess! Just don't laugh. That's all
Pure nonsense. Well, if you want to, drink some vodka.

(*She offers him a glass.*)

WAYFARER: (*He shakes his head negatively.*)

(*Silence.*)

JULIA:
Robert, you know I am very unhappy!
I've spent all of my life here in the forest.
My mother died long ago. My father's surly,
Always tramping through the woods, for days
On end, out hunting, or on business. Guests
Come here but rarely—and then who? The sexton,
The gardener from Voznitsins', and the miller . . .
It's only in summer that ladies and gentlemen visit
Otradnoye—but how can I go up to them?
I'm so ashamed; I don't know how to speak
Their language; they laugh at me; I'm not at all
Well educated . . . But I simply cannot
Live this life any more! I'm bored, I'm bored!
I feel the need of something else. I like
Nice clothes and luxury. I want to go
To theatres and to balls. I want to chat
In drawing rooms. I'm sure I would know how
To seem no sillier than any countess.
Really, I am quite beautiful! My eyes
Are large, my ears are small, and I have legs
That are elegant and a body smooth as marble!

I'd hold my own with any other countess
With all her airs and ingratiating ways!
I'd quickly learn to play the pianoforte
And dance all of the latest dances. I've
An innate sense of elegance. But here
Who is there to see me? Pine trees, birds,
My father and the peasants! And what do I hear?
Barking, swearing, shooting, and the howling of wolves
As they come running towards us through the snow . . .
I'd like to lean back in an easy chair
And, with a tea cup casually in hand,
Listen to amorous whisperings in French . . .
But no—I have to sweep the floors, prepare
The dinner, do the wash, and bring the water
For our horse, and to think that for all eternity
There is nothing else I'll ever know!

(*The charcoal in the stove goes out.*)

Well, I'll get married soon. To whom? A forester
Of course! Or even worse, it may well be
A miller! And then I shall put on weight,
Count bags of meal, and all night long hear
The wheels creak as the water makes them turn . . .
My unloved husband will kiss me on the cheeks
And lips—with his gross, over-heavy lips;
Sometimes he'll pet me roughly, with a sneer,
Sometimes, when he's half-drunk, he'll pull my braids!
Once children come, I'll wash their hands and cut their hair,
Cook them porridge, whip them with willow switches . . .
And slowly I'll forget my girlish dreams
Like the ends of candles that have burned out!
Oh, no! I've not the strength to think of it!

(*Silence.*)

Robert! You think that, living in the forest,
Like all the country wenches, I did not
Preserve my virtue? Now by all that's holy,
I swear to you: until this moment no one
Has ever kissed me, and there is no one
To whom I've spoken words of love. I am
Pure, as the summer sky, as water from the spring,
I would not shame the royal bed of a king.
The most malicious slanderer could not
Speak ill of me! . . . What am I waiting for?
I do not know. Perhaps I am waiting to

Find out that I'm the daughter of a count,
Waiting for some prince to come to my country
And tell me: I have been looking for you throughout
The world, and now I have found you, come with me
To my sumptuous palace and be the tsarina!
I am waiting, the years pass, I am alone,
There is no joy, nor will there be, that's clear!
And, if I tell the truth, yes, there are times
I am ashamed that I have been so chaste!
(*Silence. It grows darker and darker in the room.*)
But perhaps I am complaining without cause,
And the day that I was waiting for has come,
And Robert, you're the one who has been sent
To me to answer all my prayers! I did
Expect the prince to come in a golden coach,
With throngs of servants, followed by his retinue,
But he came on foot, alone. I did expect
He would be wearing velvet and brocade,
And he appeared in a jacket and overcoat!
I had imagined that on bended knee
He would express his love for me eloquently
In a long speech, full of passionate compliments,
But he is mute! . . . Well, still! Isn't it clear
That he's the one! How odd! Robert, answer! Did
You know that you were sent to me by Fate?
You are the one that I was waiting for!
You are the one the Lord ordained for me!
My betrothed! My beloved! My sweetheart!
Yes! I recognize your eyes, your sad
And wistful look, the slender, delicately
Bent fingers of your beautiful hands!
Robert! Robert! Tell me that I'm the one!
WAYFARER: (*He makes no response at all.*)
JULIA:
Well, no matter, listen! Whoever you are,
The one or not the one, what matter to us?
I won't find something better, and where will you
Ever meet another girl like me?
You think I'm beautiful? And young? Till now
I've never kissed a man! All of the strength
Of my virginal tenderness I'll give to you!
To you I'll give my innocence, as if
You were my fiancé, my husband, my master!

I'm going to believe that you're some prince,
Traveling in disguise, who has lost his throne,
And must in the meantime conceal his name!
I shall serve you like a faithful servant,
And, like a tsarina, caress and care
For you! Believe in me! Stay here with me!
You'll spend this night as in a fairy tale!
And even you'll believe we live in a castle,
That above our bed there hangs a canopy
Of gold brocade, and that hundreds of servants
Wait zealously outside the door, that all
We do is say the word—the hall will blaze
With fire, and a chorus of musicians burst out!
Oh, how I am going to adore you,
And fondle and caress you! Your every wish
I shall fulfill! I will be passionate,
Submissive, tender, whatever you want me to be!
Upon awaking in the morning, you
Will see the daughter of a forester,
Bustling about the house. She'll offer you
Some milk. And you will think you dreamed a strange
Dream. You'll say thanks, put on your overcoat,
And go away, leaving these parts forever,
And, if you want to, you'll forget about me . . .
Robert! My prince! My lord and master! Take
Me, as though I were some precious pearl
Cast at your feet from the depths of the sea!
Take me, as the gift of a nameless fairy,
Who caught sight of you in the thick of the forest!
Take me! Possess me! I am yours, all yours!

(*She throws herself at the Wayfarer.*)

Let me squeeze against you! Give me your lips,
To press mine against yours! Give me your hands,
To put them around my waist! . . . Why don't you want to?

(*She stares fixedly at him and suddenly recoils in horror.*)

Robert! Robert! It cannot be! He's dead!

(*Once again she bends over the Wayfarer sitting immobilely in the armchair, then in fright rushes to the window.*)

He's dead! Who's there! You people! Help me! Help!

END

Carlos Among the Candles

Wallace Stevens

Written 1916
Published 1917
First performance: Wisconsin Players, New York, 1917

The stage is indistinguishable when the curtain rises.

The room represented is semi-circular. In the center, at the back, is a large round window, covered by long curtains. There is a door at the right and one at the left. Farther forward on the stage there are two long, low, wooden tables, one at the right and one at the left. The walls and the curtains over the window are of a dark reddish-purple, with a dim pattern of antique gold.

Carlos is an eccentric pedant of about forty. He is dressed in black. He wears close-fitting breeches and a close-fitting, tightly-buttoned, short coat with long tails. His hair is rumpled. He leaps upon the stage through the door at the right. Nothing is visible through the door. He has a long thin white lighted taper, which he holds high above his head as he moves, fantastically, over the stage, examining the room in which he finds himself.

When he has completed examining the room, he tip-toes to the table at the right and lights a single candle at the edge of the table nearest the front of the stage. It is a thin black candle, not less than two feet high. All the other candles are like it. They give very little light.

He speaks in a lively manner, but is over-nice in sounding his words.

As the candle begins to burn, he steps back, regarding it. Nothing else is visible on the table.

CARLOS: How the solitude of this candle penetrates me! I light a candle in the darkness. It fills the darkness with solitude, which becomes my own. I become a part of the solitude of the candle . . . of the darkness flowing over the house and into it . . . This room . . . and the profound room outside . . . Just to go through a door, and the change . . . the becoming a part, instantly, of that profounder room . . . and equally to feel it communicating, with the same persistency, its own mood, its own influence . . . and there, too, to feel the lesser influences of the shapes of things, of exhalations, sounds . . to feel the mood of the candle vanishing and the mood of the special night coming to take its place . . .

(He sighs. After a pause he pirouettes, and then continues.)

I was always affected by the grand style. And yet I have been thinking neither of mountains nor of morgues . . . To think of this light and of myself . . . it is a duty . . . Is it because it makes me think of myself in other places in such a light . . . or of other people in other places in such a light? How true that is: other people in other places in such a light . . . If I looked in at that window and saw a single candle burning in an empty room . . . but if I saw a figure . . . If, now, I felt that there was someone outside . . . The vague influence . . . the influence that clutches . . . But it is not only here and now . . . It is in the morning . . . the difference between a small window and a large window . . . a blue window and a green window . . . It is in the afternoon and in the evening . . . in effects, so drifting, that I know myself to be incalculable, since the causes of what I am are incalculable . . .

(He springs toward the table, flourishing his taper. At the end farthest from the front of the stage, he discovers a second candle, which he lights. He goes back to his former position.)

The solitude dissolves . . . The light of two candles has a meaning different from the light of one . . . and an effect different from the effect of one . . . And the proof that that is so, is that I feel the difference . . . The associations have drifted a little and changed, and I have followed in this change . . . If I see myself in other places in such a light, it is not as I saw myself before. If I see other people in other places in such a light, the people and places are different from the people and places I saw before. The solitude is gone. It is as if a company of two or three people had just separated, or as if they were about to gather. These candles are too far apart.

(He flourishes his taper above the table and finds a third candle in the center of it, which he lights.)

And yet with only two candles it would have been a cold and respectable company; for the feeling of coldness and respectability persists in the presence of three, modified a little, as if a kind of stateliness had modified into a kind of elegance . . . How far away from the isolation of the single candle, as arrogant of the vacancy around it as three are arrogant of association . . . It is no longer as if a company had just separated. It is only as if it were about to gather . . . as if one were soon to forget the room because of the people in the room . . . people tempered by the lights around them, affected by the lights around them . . . sensible that one more candle would turn this formative elegance into formative luxury.

(He lights a fourth candle. He indulges his humor.)

And the suggestion of luxury into the suggestion of magnificence.

(He lights a fifth candle.)

And the beginning of magnificence into the beginning of splendor.

(He lights a sixth candle. He sighs deeply.)

In how short a time have I been solitary, then respectable—in a company so cold as to be stately, then elegant, then conscious of luxury, even magnificence; and now I come, gradually, to the beginning of splendor. Truly, I am a modern.

(He dances around the room.)

To have changed so often and so much . . . or to have been changed . . . to have been carried by the lighting of six candles through so many lives and to have been brought among so many people . . . This grows more wonderful. Six candles burn like an adventure that has been completed. They are established. They are a city . . . six common candles . . . seven . . .

(He lights another and another, until he has lighted twelve, saying after them in turn.)

Eight, nine, ten, eleven, twelve.

(Following this, he goes on tip-toe to the center of the stage, where he looks at the candles. Their brilliance has raised his spirits to the point of gaiety. He turns from the lighted table to face the dark one at the left. He holds his taper before him.)

Darkness again . . . as if a night wind had come blowing . . . but too weakly to fling the cloth of darkness.

(He goes to the window, draws one of the curtains a little and peers out. He sees nothing.)

I had as lief look into night as look into the dark corner of a room. Darkness expels me.

(He goes forward, holding his taper high above him, until he comes to the table at the left. He finds this covered with candles, like the table at the right, and lights them, with whimsical motions, one by one. When all the candles have been lighted, he runs to the center of the stage, holding his hands over his eyes. Then he returns to the window and flings aside the curtains. The light from the window falls on the tall stalks of flowers outside. The flowers are like hollyhocks, but they are unnaturally large, of gold and silver. He speaks excitedly.)

Where now is my solitude and the lonely figure of solitude? Where now are the two stately ones that left their coldness behind them? They have taken their bareness with them. Their coldness has followed them. Here there will be silks and fans . . . the movement of arms . . . rumors of Renoir . . . coiffures . . . hands . . . scorn of Debussy . . . communications of body to body . . . There will be servants, as fat as plums, bearing pineapples from the Azores . . . because of twenty-four candles, burning together, as if their light had dispelled a phantasm, falling on silks and fans . . the movement of arms . . . The pulse of the crowd will beat out the shallow pulses . . . it will fill me.

(*A strong gust of wind suddenly blows into the room, extinguishing several of the candles on the table at the left. He runs to the table at the left and looks, as if startled, at the extinguished candles. He buries his head in his arms.*)

That, too, was phantasm . . . The night wind came into the room . . . The fans are invisible upon the floor.

(*In a burst of feeling, he blows out all the candles that are still burning on the table at the left. He crosses the stage and stands before the table at the right. After a moment he goes slowly to the back of the stage and draws the curtains over the window. He returns to the table at the right.*)

What is there in the extinguishing of light? It is like twelve wild birds flying in autumn. (*He blows out one of the candles.*) It is like an eleven-limbed oak tree, brass-colored in frost . . . Regret . . . (*He blows out another candle.*) It is like ten green sparks of a rocket, oscillating in air . . . The extinguishing of light . . . how closely regret follows it. (*He blows out another candle.*) It is like the diverging angles that follow nine leaves drifting in water, and that compose themselves brilliantly on the polished surface. (*He blows out another candle.*) It is like eight pears in a nude tree, flaming in twilight . . . The extinguishing of light is like that. The season is sorrowful. The air is cold. (*He blows out another candle.*) It is like the six Pleiades, and the hidden one, that makes them seven. (*He blows out another candle.*) It is like the seven Pleiades, and the hidden one, that makes them six. (*He blows out another candle.*) The extinguishing of light is like the five purple palmations of cinquefoil withering . . . It is full of incipiencies of darkness . . . of desolation that rises as a feeling rises . . . Imagination wills the five purple palmations of cinquefoil. But in this light they have the appearance of withering . . . To feel and, in the midst of feeling, to imagine . . . (*He blows out another candle.*) The extinguishing of light is like the four posts of a cadaver, two at its head and two at its feet, to-wit: its arms and legs. (*He blows out another candle.*) It is like three peregrins, departing. (*He blows out another candle.*) It is like heaven and earth in the eye of the disbeliever. (*He blows out another candle. He dances around the room. He returns to the single candle that remains burning.)* The extinguishing of light is like that old Hesper, clapped upon by clouds. *(He stands in front of the candle, so as to obscure it.)* The spikes of his light bristle around the edge of the bulk. The spikes bristle among the clouds and behind them. There is a spot where he was bright in the sky . . . It remains fixed a little in the mind.

(He opens the door at the right. Outside, the night is as blue as water. He crosses the stage and opens the door at the left. Once more he flings aside the curtains. He extinguishes his taper. He looks out. He speaks with elation.)

Oh, ho! Here is matter beyond invention.

(He springs through the window. Curtain.)

END

Requiem

Leonid Andreyev

Written 1913-1916
Published 1917
First performance: Komissarzhevsky Theatre, Moscow, December 17, 1916
Translated by Daniel Gerould

It all takes place in the void.

The replica of a small theatre.
  The left side of the stage is occupied by a raised platform, or small stage, on which the actors perform—a wide scaffolding, divided in the very middle by a wall of theatre flats. The left side represents the inner sanctum of the small theatre, its backstage; on the right, the stage action is carried out. Both of these parts are equally visible, but on the left side the lighting is sparse and shadows prevail, and the movements are dim—the right side, on the contrary, is illuminated by the bright glare of the footlights, it lends itself to loud speech, measured and precise movements. But that's the whole problem!
  There are no spectators in the small theatre.

Puppets *take their place, flat wooden figures, cut out of thin planks by a carpenter and painted by a painter. In two flat rows, sitting on imaginary chairs, they surround the small stage in a semicircle, they watch relentlessly with painted eyes, they do not move, they do not breathe, they keep totally quiet. The glare from the footlights is reflected on their dead rouged faces, it gives them an illusion of life; wavering, it appears to make them waver. Striking against the flat figures, the sounds of loud speech also come back to the small stage—it seems that the puppets are talking, laughing, even crying.*
  The Manager and the Actors call them the spectators.

PLAY

The night before the first performance. Dark and desolate. The small stage is shrouded in gloom, and only a faint light from a few bulbs illuminates the space between the small stage and the spectators, dimly outlining their painted faces, their immobilely wooden figures. Two people are quietly carrying on a conversation: the Director and the Artist. The artist is restless, a bit too effusive, somewhat overactive. The director is taciturn and somber.

ARTIST: Forgive me, my dear colleague, for breaking in on you like this at night. Really, it's so desolate here. But you, my dear colleague, are a director and involved in art yourself, you'll understand my excitement, as an artist. I'd like to take another look at those amazing figures, created by my brush. Couldn't they, my dear colleague, be more brightly lit?

DIRECTOR: Out of the question.

ARTIST: But why not? It seems to me that that one over there, the third from the end, is not quite finished. Two or three quick touches. Oh, you don't know what just a single stroke means, when it has inspiration to back it up!

DIRECTOR: Out of the question.

ARTIST: I'd just like to touch up the cheek. It seems to me that it's not sufficiently bright or rounded. He's actually a heavy-set man, you understand, my dear colleague!

DIRECTOR: Out of the question. I am waiting for the Theatre Manager and His Highness.

ARTIST: (*Bows respectfully.*) Ah-ha, and His Highness! Then that's another story, and I say no more. I say no more, my dear colleague. I am quite sure that His Highness, more than anyone else, will appreciate my labors. They told me we don't need live spectators in the theatre, we're afraid of the noise and the rowdiness that the crowd always brings with it. Isn't that what I was told?

DIRECTOR: Yes, that's what you were told.

ARTIST: But, they added, we don't like to be in the theatre all alone, amidst empty seats and dark empty boxes. Design spectators for us, but draw them so that they totally resemble live ones, so that the good actors, who, regrettably, are overly fond of the crowd, won't notice the substitution and will boast triumphantly about the full house for the benefit performance. Isn't that right, my dear colleague?

DIRECTOR: Yes, that's right.

ARTIST: A brilliant caprice! A brilliant whim! Only in a head circled by a crown could such a fascinating bit of madness be born! The theatre full—and no one there! No one there—and the theatre full! Fascinating! Well, how about it, my dear colleague: I really brought it off, didn't I?

DIRECTOR: You brought it off.

ARTIST: I think I did. Oh, my dear colleague, you are too apathetic. If I were in your place, I'd jump with joy. Really, they are so life-like—you understand, so life-like that the Lord God himself could be taken in and honor them as his own creation. And what if suddenly he really were taken in? No, just you think, my dear colleague: suddenly taken in, he summons them to the *last judgment* and for the first time—just think, for the first time!—he's in a quandary, confronted with the question: who are they—the sinful or the righteous? The wooden ones—who are they: the sinful or the righteous?

DIRECTOR: Now that's philosophy.

ARTIST: Yes, yes, you're right. Down with philosophy and long live art for art's sake! I don't care about the *last judgment*, the only judgment that matters to me is the one made by His Highness and Herr Manager. I must admit, I'm a bit afraid of your manager: he is a very strange gentleman. And aren't you afraid of him?

DIRECTOR: No.

ARTIST: But he pays very generously. Doesn't he?

DIRECTOR: He is paid very generously himself.

ARTIST: Really? Then His Highness is a very rich man? Well, of course, how can I ask such a question? The theatre belongs to His Highness, and those *spectators* don't pay any admission. (*He points with his hand to the painted spectators and laughs.*) Even I cannot bring them to that point of perfection. Now can I? (*But his laugh dies out all by itself. The Director doesn't say a word. Bending over, the Artist whispers.*) Of course, there's nothing funny about it. You're right, my dear colleague. But won't you tell me now that we're completely alone—I think that for ten miles around you won't find a single living creature in the vicinity of this theatre—now that we're completely alone, won't you tell me as a friend: what does all of this mean? Of course, it's a brilliant whim . . . but what does it all mean? To be quite frank, I'm somewhat afraid, or rather I feel a kind of strange and unpleasant excitement. Why does His Highness wear a black mask?

DIRECTOR: All of Europe knows his face, and he does not want to be recognized.

ARTIST: All of Europe?

DIRECTOR: And America.

ARTIST: And America? So who is he then?

DIRECTOR: I do not know.

ARTIST: You're so taciturn, my dear colleague, that I'm falling into a state of despair. Understand that it's awful for me, or rather I feel a kind of strange and unpleasant excitement. Why haven't I once seen any of your *actors*?

DIRECTOR: You know one of them.

ARTIST: Really? Who is that?

DIRECTOR: You.

ARTIST: Oh, stop it; that's an old and silly play on words. Yes, yes, we are actors, and life is a theatre, and the spectators . . . I beg your pardon: but, perhaps, you've got wooden actors too? Now that would be a fine thing. . . .

DIRECTOR: No. They suffer.

ARTIST: Yes, yes, of course. But are they paid a salary? Oh, my dear colleague: I am paid a salary—therefore I exist, that's not even philosophy . . . But doors were slamming somewhere.

DIRECTOR: That's the Manager arriving.

ARTIST: Oh, good heavens! There are doors slamming again. I'm afraid my presence here at this hour may seem out of place to Herr Manager or to His

Highness. I haven't even had the honor of being introduced . . .

DIRECTOR: The Manager is a very amiable man.

ARTIST: And what about His Highness? My hands are growing sweaty from excitement. I shall call you to witness, my dear colleague. I shall call you to witness!

MANAGER: (*Voice offstage.*) Careful, Your Highness, there are some steps here.

(*Two men enter: His Highness, a tall man, wrapped in a black coat, a black half-mask over his face. Behind him, slightly hunched over in deference, comes The Manager, likewise tall and likewise dressed in black. The Manager's face, clean-shaven, like an actor's, is gloomy, but energetic. Given the slight mobility of the features, it reflects the play of his soul only by dark shadows. He holds himself with dignity; at times, more in the tone of his voice than in the sense of the words themselves, there can be heard an undercurrent of scorn, almost hostility toward the eminent guest.*)

MAN IN THE MASK: It's dark in here.

MANAGER: I'll have the lights turned on, Your Highness.

MAN IN THE MASK No, wait. Who are those two?

ARTIST & DIRECTOR: (*Bow.*)

MANAGER: (*Quietly.*) Those are my co-workers, Your Highness. The somber one is the director, he's one of ours. He keeps quiet and does his job. He's so adept at keeping quiet that Your Highness with that love of silence, which I have made bold to notice, will undoubtedly grace him with your favor. And that other one is the artist. He'll die of extreme longing if I don't present him to Your Highness. Will you permit me?

MAN IN THE MASK: Present him.

MANAGER: (*Aloud.*) Your Highness, allow me to present to you my highly esteemed co-worker, the famous artist, a genius, whose brush works true miracles. He gave our theatre its *spectators*. (*The Artist bows. And bows again.*)

MAN IN THE MASK: Are you a genius?

ARTIST: Your Highness! . . .

MAN IN THE MASK: But why are your cheeks red—is your genius so well fed? You eat too much meat. That's not good for you. I'll send my doctor around to see you.

ARTIST: Your Highness! . . . (*The Man in the Mask turns away and the Artist leaves, bowing. After having indicated his delight to the Director by means of gestures, he quickly disappears.*)

HIS HIGHNESS: Do you have everything ready, Herr Manager?

MANAGER: As you ordered, Your Highness. How do you like the theatre itself? It cost me no small effort to find a suitable building on the outskirts of the capital. There are human beings out there somewhere . . . (*he points with his hand indefinitely*) but on either side there is wilderness and night. Only an old brick wall separates us from that wilderness and night.

HIS HIGHNESS: But the night penetrates even through the stones.

MANAGER: Yes, the night penetrates even through the stones. Once people lived and died in this house: here where we are standing there was previously someone's bedroom. Then the building grew old, and was left to die. As a matter of fact, this is already a dead house, and they were planning to tear it down when the money from Your Highness gave it new life. Now it is a theatre.

HIS HIGHNESS: This seems to be the second floor—but what's below us?

MANAGER: I cannot precisely say, Your Highness, empty rooms, I think. The same as above us—the doors were nailed shut, and I did not consider it necessary to open them. We'll be giving only one performance, I assume.

HIS HIGHNESS: Yes, only one. I like this theatre. You understood what I wanted. The bedroom was here? I believe that's what you said. I like that. You could say that they are still asleep and see it all in a dream. You are a clever man, Herr Manager.

MANAGER: (Bows.)

HIS HIGHNESS: This is the stage. . . . And what's that back there, behind the partition?

MANAGER: That's the backstage. Out here is where they perform; back there is where they get ready for the performance, where they live and where they also perform.

HIS HIGHNESS: And where will you put the orchestra?

MANAGER: As you ordered, Your Highness—offstage. They won't be visible.

HIS HIGHNESS: They won't be visible. Yes—it is essential that between the *actors* and *those* over there no *living* thing be interposed. Understand me—if as much as a mouse runs along here, it will spoil the whole beauty of the show for us. Out here it should be empty and deathly still.

MANAGER: As in the grave?

HIS HIGHNESS: The dead speak.

MANAGER: As in your heart, Your Highness?

HIS HIGHNESS: And in yours, Herr Manager. Now show me *those* over there.

MANAGER: (*Turns to the silent Director.*) Go and carry out my orders. Bring up the lights on the *spectators*. (*The Director withdraws. His Highness and the Manager, their heads inclined, like masters of their trade, unhurriedly scrutinize the* spectators.)

HIS HIGHNESS: In this dim light I find *them* pleasing. They resemble living people. *That one* over there positively stirred when you praised the artist, Herr Manager.

MANAGER: And *that one* over there positively gets to his feet when he hears Your Highness's voice. (*The two of them laugh quietly. Suddenly bright lights come on full and fall on the wooden spectators, mercilessly exposing their flat, wooden faces, the pitiful splashes of motley colors, the naive tomfoolery devoid of any shame.*)

HIS HIGHNESS: And are these the *spectators* at our theatre?

MANAGER: Yes, these are the *spectators* at our theatre. But are you surprised, Your Highness? You really didn't expect this?

HIS HIGHNESS: Yes, I am surprised. And do you think that our actors will believe in them?

MANAGER: Our *actors* will believe in them.

HIS HIGHNESS: In that wood and red coloring?—in that pitiful smear by a talentless paint-slinger—in that naive tomfoolery devoid of shame? Never, Herr Manager, your actors will hiss you. Those *puppets* are not even fit to be scarecrows in a garden, they wouldn't even fool a sparrow!

MANAGER: But our *actors* will believe in them. Oh, Your Highness, isn't that the whole point of our performance? We made up our minds to have a good laugh, but would there be anything to laugh at if these *puppets* were . . . no worse than we are? Only a genius at mediocrity, like my famous *artist*, who has poured all his immortal soul into his creation, could produce such a combination: immortality at being a total nonentity. Take a good look, Your Highness: at first glance there's nothing but wood and paint; but later on—*they* start to look about them! Later still—don't you hear a kind of strange wooden pulse beating? A bit after that—and then someone's wooden voice. . . .

HIS HIGHNESS: You may well be right. And don't you think that you too will believe in them?

MANAGER: I will?

HIS HIGHNESS: Yes, you will. By the end of the performance, of course.

MANAGER: I will? You're having a little joke, aren't you, Your Highness?

HIS HIGHNESS: Yes, I'm joking. You interest me, Herr Manager. If my question doesn't strike you as indiscreet: where is your wife, Herr Manager? You are a man not in the first flush of youth.

MANAGER: She died, Your Highness.

HIS HIGHNESS: And your children?

MANAGER: They died, Your Highness.

HIS HIGHNESS: And your friends?

MANAGER: They died, Your Highness.

HIS HIGHNESS: You're all alone?

MANAGER: Exactly like you, Your Highness . . . if you will pardon my indiscreet observation.

HIS HIGHNESS: Yes. You are forgetting yourself.

MANAGER: (*Without saying a word, he bows. Silence.*)

HIS HIGHNESS: Have the lights brought up on stage.

MANAGER: (*Shouting.*) Bring up the lights on stage!

(*A pillar of bright light moves across to the small stage. The* spectators *seem to fade out, melt into the semi-darkness, grow vaguely animated.)*

HIS HIGHNESS: You have only a table and chair on stage. . . . Is that really sufficient for the performance?

MANAGER: Quite sufficient, Your Highness. The rest they will imagine.

HIS HIGHNESS: And that strange plant? Judging by its spikes I'd say it was a cactus, if there weren't something suspiciously alive and overly malicious about its sinuous curves. In its gaze. . . .

MANAGER: You've noticed that it looks at you?

HIS HIGHNESS: Yes. In its gaze there is something treacherous, it hides, as though lying in wait. It is clever . . . but what does it mean?

MANAGER: Whatever you wish, Your Highness: sorrow and joy, life and death. In spring it resembles a garden, in winter a cemetery; to a king it recalls his crown. It is a stage convention, whose aim is to facilitate the workings of the imagination and to give the performance naturalness and indispensable emotional force.

HIS HIGHNESS: I find you most likable, Herr Manager. Tomorrow I shall listen to your music with pleasure and take a look at the *actors*—they must be no less interesting than everything else that you have already shown me.

MANAGER: But why tomorrow?

HIS HIGHNESS: It is night now.

MANAGER: Yes, it is night now.

HIS HIGHNESS: Your musicians are asleep.

MANAGER: But isn't night really a stage convention? The musicians are ready, Your Highness, and await instructions.

MAN IN THE MASK: (*Shrugs his shoulders.*) You are a sorcerer, Herr Manager. I am listening.

MANAGER: (*Bows and says in a low voice:*) Bring up the music.

(*The orchestra plays offstage. The tall Man in the Mask and the Manager listen attentively; the Man in the Mask has leaned his arm on the edge of the small stage, inclined his head and, apparently, sunk into a deep reverie. The Manager stands as though he were lending an ear to his companion's thoughts. The Tall Man breathes a sigh.*)

HIS HIGHNESS: That is very joyful music.

MANAGER: Yes, Your Highness, very joyful.

HIS HIGHNESS: And yet there's a touch of sorrow in it too. Your wife was beautiful, was she, Herr Manager?

MANAGER: Yes, Your Highness.

HIS HIGHNESS: And yet there's a touch of melancholy in it too. Your wife died, did she, Herr Manager?

MANAGER: Yes, Your Highness.

HIS HIGHNESS: And yet there's also a mortal weariness in it, and fright, and a moaning of the homeless wind, and a faint entreaty for help. . . . Your children died, did they, Herr Manager? But why are you keeping silent? Am I mistaken—or is that your theatre's joyful theme?

MANAGER: You are not mistaken. That is our theatre's joyful theme. If you pay close attention, you will make it out: it is the usual music that is played at all the balls. It makes you feel like dancing when you hear it.

HIS HIGHNESS: Yes, it makes you feel like dancing. You've changed the tune so skillfully that the transposition is scarcely noticeable. But that will do. I don't feel like dancing.

MANAGER: (*Bows and shouts.*) That will do. (*The music ceases. Silence.*)

MAN IN THE MASK: (*With a movement of his head indicates the painted spectators.*) They should be pleased. Why don't they applaud?

MANAGER: There aren't any actors here yet.

HIS HIGHNESS: What about us?

MANAGER: Your Highness is in fine humor and permits himself a little joke. But don't you want to take a look at the real actors who will make the reputation of our theatre tomorrow? They are at your orders.

MAN IN THE MASK: Right now? But now it's the dead of night.

MANAGER: Night is only a convention. If you'll be so kind as to take a seat—the performance will take quite a bit of time—I shall parade my actors before you. Each of them, brightly lit and in the costume and make-up in which he plays his role, will pass across the stage. . . .

MAN IN THE MASK: No, I shall stand. I am watching.

MANAGER: (*Gives the order in a low voice.*) Bring on the actors.

(*The lights suddenly go out, and for a few moments total darkness reigns. Then at the rear of the small stage an aureole of light comes on full, within which are two figures: a young man and young woman in romantic medieval costumes. Their arms about each other, with a frozen expression of happiness and torment on their faces, they slowly pass across the stage with a gliding step and vanish through the door that leads backstage; and the light follows them. All the while as they move along, their eyes look straight ahead of them, their faces deathly and strangely immobile, like those of corpses.*)

MANAGER: (*Explains.*) Those are the lovers. I deliberately dressed them in medieval costumes: it's more in keeping with love than our disgustingly prosaic modern dress. They die at the end of the second act.

MAN IN THE MASK: No so loud!

MANAGER: They can't hear us. They both die at the end of the second act.

(*Again the lights come on full at the end of the small stage, and there appears the figure of a happy-go-lucky man-about-town in a tail coat. With a frozen grimace of laughter on his deathly-pale face, he slowly passes across the small stage, looking straight ahead of him all the time. In the buttonhole of his cutaway, there is a huge red rose the size of a ripening head of cabbage.)*

MANAGER: (*Explains.*) There goes the most happy-go-lucky man in the world. He lives on laughter; smirks, not blood, flow through his veins, and where most people have hearts that beat, he keeps a hilariously funny, a delightfully absurd anecdote pumping away.

MAN IN THE MASK: Does he die?

MANAGER: Like all of us, Your Highness.

(Again the lights come on full. There passes across the stage, or rather majestically floats over it, a tall, proud man, getting on in years, with a handsome clean-shaven face. In his ossified majesty he resembles a ponderously moving statue.)

MANAGER: Here comes a brilliant actor. Emperors and heroes are his particular forte. He does away with himself at the end of the third act.

MAN IN THE MASK: People like that usually cut their throats with a razor.

MANAGER: You are mistaken, Your Highness: he blows his brains out.

(The actor vanishes. A tall blind woman, her emaciated arms outstretched, passes into the aureole of light. Grief is imprinted on her face.)

MAN IN THE MASK: (*Exclaims softly.*) Oh, what grief! Her eyes are red with weeping. Who is she looking for?

MANAGER: She is looking for her son.

MAN IN THE MASK: And she won't find him, will she?

MANAGER: He died. I beg Your Highness to pay attention to the next character. He is a *prophet*. A valuable addition to the troupe.

(A young man, with an energetic expression on his ardent, emaciated face that seems as though it has been consumed by fire. Shackled by a corpse-like immobility, like all the others, he is bursting with latent motion. His clothes are torn, and on his chest and face there is dried blood.)

MANAGER: One of my most talented actors.

MAN IN THE MASK: But why do they stare so?

MANAGER: They do not see.

MAN IN THE MASK: But why do they walk with such a strange, gliding step, like ghosts?

MANAGER: They *are* ghosts, Your Highness. They are asleep and dreaming. Even for Your Highness I would not have dared disturb the living on such a desolate night as this. (*For some time, without saying a word, they look into each other's eyes. The Man in the Mask smiles, the Manager lowers his eyes.)*

MAN IN THE MASK: And what about us? Aren't we asleep and dreaming too?

MANAGER: If no one sees us dreaming, it means that we are not asleep. But aren't you permitting yourself a little joke, Your Highness? And I am afraid that this procession of ghosts has worn you out. Allow me to present the rest of the actors to you tomorrow, and for now I shall limit myself to what constitutes my pride and joy. These are my *extras*. After prolonged efforts I have succeeded in getting them to resemble one another like peas in a pod. It is a very funny spectacle. Bring on the *extras!*

(One after the other there pass across the stage dozens of absolutely identical human beings with gray faces devoid of expression, so alike as to be ludicrous.)

MAN IN THE MASK: I cannot decide which please me the most: your spectators or *these*. Bravo, Herr Manager! *(He claps with tiny little hands encased in black gloves.)*

MANAGER: *(Bows.)* Skillfully done, isn't it? Now that is all, Your Highness.

(Silence. The extras pass across the stage. Suddenly the lights go out and then go on again at the end of the small stage. The Manager appears surprised.)

MAN IN THE MASK: *(Laughs quietly.)* No, I believe there is something more, now, isn't there? Evidently, you were trying to conceal something, Herr Manager, weren't you?

MANAGER: There is nothing more.

MAN IN THE MASK: You think not?

(A moment of darkness and quiet, in which the breathing of the Manager can be heard. At the end of the small stage, from where the actors appeared, there is a pale sepulchral light, a vague illumination, as though hundreds of glowworms or wet rotten stumps had kindled their own radiance. Woven from these threads of light there arises the vague, undulating image of a woman who once was beautiful.)

MANAGER: *(His voice from out of the darkness:)* Good Lord, the image is moving!

MAN IN THE MASK: Take a look at your wooden spectators, Herr Manager: even they are excited. Who is that passing across the stage?

MANAGER: Leave me alone.

(The image moves.)

MAN IN THE MASK: Or are there actors in your troupe who are not known to you, Herr Manager? But it seems to me that this one is known to you.

(He laughs. The light goes out. Silence. Darkness. And when the light of the lamps

again comes on full, everything appears in its place: the empty small stage, the painted spectators, and in between—the tall Man in the Black Mask and the Manager. But the Manager is very pale—almost like a ghost.)

MAN IN THE MASK: (*Speaks solicitously.*) Are you worn out, Herr Manager? Have I exhausted you? You are so pale.

MANAGER: A slight indisposition.

MAN IN THE MASK: But then it is imperative that you receive medical treatment, my dear colleague. I shall send my doctor around to see you.

MANAGER: (*Bows.*) I am flattered by Your Highness's attention. But what are your commands as to where to reserve you a place for tomorrow's show? Here?

(He points to an empty chair, standing in the same row as the painted spectators. For some time they look at one another.)

MAN IN THE MASK: (*Speaks slowly.*) No.

MANAGER: But. . . .

MAN IN THE MASK: No. I shall come only at the end of the performance.

MANAGER: When the actor blows his brains out?

MAN IN THE MASK: Yes, at approximately that point.

MANAGER: (*Grabs him by the hand in a violent state of excitement and stammers.*) But I implore you! . . . Come earlier. Come at the beginning . . . You frighten me . . . Who are you? You are like the stranger who came to Mozart, ordered him to write a Requiem and never appeared again, but the *Requiem* kept running through Mozart's head . . . to the very end. Aren't you the unknown visitor who called on Mozart?

MAN IN THE MASK: No.

MANAGER: You're lying.

MAN IN THE MASK: And you're forgetting yourself.

MANAGER: (*Whispers threateningly.*) Start talking, or I'll rip the mask off your face. (*Silence.*)

MAN IN THE MASK: (*Answers calmly and cheerfully.*) If that is the performance we are giving, then the show has not started yet, has it, Herr Manager? What is the matter with you? You know perfectly well why I came to see you, and I can distinctly hear my gold clinking in your pocket. Or haven't I paid you everything I owe you? Tell me, and you will receive payment in full. But you are very pale, my dear colleague.

MANAGER: (*Gloomily.*) Forgive me, Your Highness. But ever since I have had to deal with the actors. . . .

MAN IN THE MASK: You overstep the bounds too freely . . . I understand you. So then—until tomorrow. I hope to see you fully recovered by tomorrow—I am so pleased with you that it would be a shame, a terrible shame. But in any case I shall send my doctor around. Yes, yes, don't raise any objections:

he will be useful—if not for you, then for your actors—to certify their death. Without that they really can't be buried, now can they? Although I do hope it will be a theatrical death, don't you? The kind of death following which the dead take their friends and mistresses to a lively little tavern and spend the entire night drinking there till dawn. Not one thing more, Herr Manager, you are such a joker, I know you. . . . No, no, don't bother to see me out, I'll find the way myself. Goodbye.

(*His last words already drift out of the darkness. The Manager, as though he had been frozen in the posture of a respectful bow, slowly straightens his shoulders, throws back his pale head and looks after the departing figure. Out there first one door and then another slams shut—and still another, as though the wind had caught them, and they close with a loud bang that slowly fades away in the distance. Silence.*)

MANAGER: (*Yells with sudden sharpness.*) Hey, you! Come here!

(*Out of the darkness, like a heavier clot condensed from it, there appears the Director.*)

DIRECTOR: (*Waits silently.*)
MANAGER: You may go. I'll put the lights out myself. There's no one else there?
DIRECTOR: No one.
MANAGER: (*Angrily.*) I know your little tricks! Are you still here?
DIRECTOR: (*Keeps silent.*)
MANAGER: I'll show you who is master here. Bring up the lights on the stage and leave. I want to be alone. Do you hear . . . or have you gone deaf? Leave.
DIRECTOR: (*Disappears.*)

(*In a moment the footlights come on full and illuminate the small stage. And once again the successive slamming of many doors can be heard—in the distance someone is leaving for a long time.*)

MANAGER: (*Listening.*) One—two—three. . . . How strange: why is it there are so many dooors? Still another . . . and another. Now he's gone. (*Exhausted, he looks around. He passes between the small stage and the painted spectators and stops in front of one of them, looks at him for a long time, with his hands thrust in his pockets.*) Yes, they live in the dark. But just who does that one look like so botched up? Some one of my friends. What a botch! (*He shakes his head for a long time. He moves away and climbs up the stairs to the small stage, paces back and forth, alone in the illuminated space.*) You can breathe only when you're alone. (*Looks around.*) Yes, the light is sufficient. They are just as visible as is necessary. A fine light. But why are there so many doors here? They kept slamming as though he were stepping out into infinity. That's because it is night and sounds are absurdly loud. Because it is night. (*He straightens the table and chair.*) It'll be better that way. Yes, a fine light. Let's rest a bit. (*He sits down at the table, facing the painted spectators.*) Let's rest. (*He examines his hand.*) And yet, how violently my hand is trembling. My hand. How old my hand has become. Wrinkles, creases—row after row of furrows made by the plough. (*Turns his hand palm up.*) My happiness is here somewhere—it must be here in this line—it is frightfully short. Happiness . . . (*He grows lost in thought. He shakes his head resolutely and speaks aloud.*) Let's rest. I like it here. I love the stage, when it is still empty, but the lights are already on; I love the empty ballroom before the beginning of the ball; I love the lowered curtain, downcast eyes, unspoken speech. Perhaps tomorrow I shall quit the stage, like a hissed actor, but today I am waiting for something. All my life I have been waiting, and the ball has not yet started, and someone does not come and gives no answer, and my heart has already grown weary. Now I shall begin to cry. I shall scream out loud, I may even start to sob—and no one will hear me. I am alone here. And my scream will be like the scream of one asleep and dreaming; even the pillow cannot hear him; and if you bent your ear next to his mouth, even then you wouldn't hear: the dreamer cries out but his cry is stifled within him. Who knows? Who can say?—Perhaps the dead do howl in their graves, but all is quiet in the cemetery. Who knows —perhaps I died a long time ago, and all this is only the fantasy of my dead brain . . . or of the void that it has peopled. And the guard with a lantern makes his rounds of the cemetery and thinks: "How quiet it is in my domain, I shall add my dream to their eternal dream." No, it's not worth crying over. (*He keeps silent and rubs his chilled fingers to warm them. He raises his head.*) I shall not express my sufferings by tears. Nor shall I give voice to my sufferings by screaming; no matter how I cry out or spew forth ponderous words—only a sea of silence, a barren sea of stillness and reticence, a smooth glassy surface of non-being will hold up the mirror image of my unspoken grief, of my bitter and frightful sorrow. But who would ever believe an actor? Not you, surely, my wooden friends, who listen so attentively and tactfully, with such deep understanding and thoughtfulness? I am alone here. He came to me in the night. There is his gold. (*He throws a pile of gold coins on the table.*) He came to me in the night. And black was that night, and black were his mask and cloak, and black the treacherous idea he proposed I carry out . . . I feel the treachery in his cold stare. There is his gold. What does he want? His spirit is restless, and his speech arrogant, and his irony blunt, and his schemes frightful, and he himself suffers in silence—who is he? (*Silence.*) And who am I? (*Silence.*) Oh, how desolate the night is. Never since the world began has there been such a desolate night as this, its gloom is frightful, its silence fathomless, and I am utterly alone. I listen for a door to bang. No, not a sound. So many doors, but no one comes, no one calls, and no voice of any living creature. (*Cries out loudly.*) Mercy! Mercy!

(*Silence. The Manager looks nervously around, waits for at least an answering echo, but the silence and gloom remain unbroken. He holds his head in his hands and keeps silent.*)

END